So You Shall Know the Truth

Books by the Same Author

Balanced Yoga: The Twelve-Week Programme
ISBN: 978-81-7822-315-5

Practical Wisdom
ISBN: 978-81-7822-363-6

Truth Will Set You Free
ISBN: 978-81-7822-314-8

Svāmi Pūrṇā

So You Shall Know the Truth

A Collection of Discourses

New Age Books

New Delhi (India)

So You Shall Know the Truth

Published by
NEW AGE BOOKS
A-44, Naraina Industrial Area, Phase-I
New Delhi–110 028 (INDIA)
E-mail: nab@newagebooksindia.com
Website: www.newagebooksindia.com

ISBN: 978-81-7822-397-1

First Edition: Delhi, 2013

Printed and published by
RP Jain for New Age Books
A-44, Naraina Industrial Area
Phase-1, New Delhi 110 028. India

Contents

Foreword

At various stages of our lives questions emerge that require attention as we seek more knowledge and meaning. What is Truth? How can I attain true understanding in this lifetime? How can I understand and integrate profound spiritual concepts yet continue with my practical mundane duties in this world of maya in a spirit of joyful and selfless seva or service? Where can I find a clear explanation of the authentic Sanskrit texts and literature and apply this understanding? How do I grasp in this lifetime the keys to mindful living based on tested perennial wisdom and values? How can I be sure of the integrity and authenticity of the ancient teachings and guidance?

Sri Sri Svāmi Pūrṇa Maharaj or Svāmi Pūrṇa is a Sat Guru — a true living Teacher — who explains in a real sense the profound spiritual tradition that has perennial and universal relevance for all of humanity. Indeed Svāmi Pūrṇa represents universal knowledge that cuts across all barriers making him a true world living Teacher and Master. As I have mentioned before in other publications, when we define teachers they can fall into one of two categories, that is:

- Those who have information, theoretical and book knowledge — who gather many facts and figures — who have some achievement in life and recognition in the world through scholarly presence, yet do not practise what they teach; or

- Teachers who have attained great knowledge and wisdom — through traditional spiritual training or enlightenment and through the practice and implementation of the teachings in their lives — and who have lived and continue to live according to the principles that they teach.

In this selection of discourses various key concepts for an approach to living are explored. The discourses are based on their true Vedic and Sanskrit origin. The selection enables the reader to understand the significance of integrating spiritual understanding in daily life and achieving balance. They represent a guide in the individual's search for universal truth, joy and spiritual fulfilment. When Svāmi Pūrṇa gives a discourse he deals with diverse groups, different nationalities, religions and backgrounds and he is faced with many different cultures. Through his guidance he leads them to a clearer and fuller dimension of life that is relevant all over the world. Some of the selected pieces are discourses on a chosen topic or subject: others are in the form of a specific question and answer session typical of the traditional approach by real teachers of such living knowledge. All of them have on-going practical significance for all of us as we experience the ups and downs of life and try to live in the spirit of practical spirituality. To assist readers vital terms are listed in the Glossary and are explained more fully throughout the selection.

'So You Shall Know the Truth' includes chosen recent discourses that again demonstrate Svāmi Pūrṇa's unique, insightful and precious teachings, originally given in the authentic oral tradition. They have been transcribed and edited in order to reflect the ancient Vedic wisdom and modern day relevance. The use of illustrations and stories provide additional richness, while also reminding us of the eternal wisdom that is available for those on the path. The discourses include answers to some of life's key questions and direct the seeker of truth on a positive path to achieve more balance, fulfilment and meaning. As with all of Svāmiji's teachings there is no mistaking the key message that responsibility for self and one's own happiness is crucial to a balanced and healthy life and to real understanding. The explanation of such fundamental issues through the discourses offers readers a real opportunity to understand their message. Some may already be aware of the works of Svāmi Pūrṇa and enjoy the endorsement that this selection provides in relation to other works: for others this may be the first taste of such knowledge. For all readers there will be a unique pleasure in participating in the clear understanding found in this edition.

Once again I am honored to have worked with such precious knowledge and to have assisted with the editing of the discourses with Petra Kues at Adhyatmik Foundation. We believe that we are privileged to have the opportunity to share this understanding at a time in the world where more enlightenment is vital.

In my view the accessible style and teachings set out in 'So You Shall Know the Truth' clearly evidence the value of a way of life that can be embarked upon whatever one's age, stage in life or background and wherever one lives in this world. They can be read again and again and, with each reading, offer more perception and wisdom.

Where further information is sought I would suggest that it would be helpful to follow up any questions by further reading or by contacting us for guidance.

DR LINDA S SPEDDING
Vice President
ADHYATMIK FOUNDATION, INC
London
www.adhyatmikfoundation.org

August 2012

Chapter

1 Body Politics

In the Vedic tradition all faculties of your body, including your organs, are of equal importance and need to be in balance. When all are working in balance the result is wellness. A Havan, a fire ceremony, used to be performed to invoke the assistance and energy of the Highest One to achieve this balance.*

There are powerful mantras which concentrate on the individual organs and faculties; these mantras can become very useful tools to achieve strengthening and balancing of the particular organ or faculty. In general, each mantra is to be repeated seven times, preferably in the morning.

- Om prana prana - Prana is your life force and it will determine your departure from this earth. Strengthening your prana, your life force, will assist in longevity. Yogis for instance can determine their time of death through management of their prana. Depending on your level of evolution at the moment of leaving your body, prana can exit through any of the seven gates of the body. This mantra is helpful in fortifying your prana.
- Om wak- wak - This is a mantra to refine your individual speech, to make your speech pleasant and powerful. It can enhance the power of speech to a point where your words are very persuasive.
- Om chakchu chakchu -This mantra focuses on the eye, on your vision. It is by invoking the Sun

energy that you can make your eye 'bright', meaning that you do not only see all worldly and mundane things, but you are also able to see through the Third Eye, to see beyond the physical. In the Bhagavad Gita Krishna gives the gift of the cosmic vision to Arjuna: "I grant you the Divine Eye, whereby you may see the cosmos". When you are being given the divine eye, you can really 'see'. This mantra is appropriate to open, purify and activate the spiritual eye.

- Om srotam, srotam - This is the mantra to strengthen and purify the ear, to activate your hearing of those things you do not normally hear.
- Om navhi navhi - This mantra focuses on the navel, one of the most vital parts in the body as the place where new life is connected. All communication, all nourishment is channeled through this port.
- Om hridam hridam - This mantra is to invoke and strengthen heart energy (similar to prana). The heart is so much more than just a pump that circulates the blood through the body. It is also the seat of the most powerful human emotions, including those that affect the entire body, both negatively and positively depending on the type of emotion. A feeling of 'Love' can bring a warm delightful sensation of well-being throughout the body. Terms like 'heartache' and 'heartbreak', describe 'heartfelt' emotions with physical sensations that occur in the heart during very strong emotional situations. Such emotions are made of pure energy, and are named after their physical effects on the body. You could even say that it is your heart that defines you. The heart has its own powerful creative intelligence and is the core of your being.
- Om kantha kantha - focuses on the throat, also a source of communication through speech and emotion (lump in the throat) and equally noteworthy since much is

processed here, both physically and emotionally and therefore needs to be protected, guarded and strengthened.

- Om sirs sirs - This mantra centers attention on the head and the very important crown chakra or Brahmahanda. Millions of cells are working here, interacting, communicating and creating electrical impulses. This is the place where genius resides. Nature has gifted the good brain to some, able to use the maximum of its potential, and, even after death, electron-cytochemical activity continues for considerable time. This mantra can also help protect the Thousand-Petaled Lotus, the Cosmos, where everything is contained, all memories, etc.
- Om bahubalam - This mantra strengthens the shoulders and is of especial importance for the elderly. Much stress can accumulate in the shoulders;therefore exercise of this area is imperative not only to strengthen, but also to keep the shoulders supple. It is a vital part of Health Management.
- Om kartalam - This mantra is effective for the hands. Hand function is an essential part in the activity of daily living. Dexterity, manifestation of endless skills of making, creating and doing, including communication with hands, both in formal sign language as well as the use of hands as visual aid to emphasize speech are all part of daily activity. The hands are the most adept and versatile tools of the human body.

Although there are many more mantras pertaining to different parts of the body, these mentioned here are the most important ones. Their daily use is highly recommended. When practicing such Mantras, do this at your own individual pace.

I have always taught people two key instructions: do not compete and do not compare. Unfortunately these two categories are part of the human culture, whether in schools, at work or at home. It is my very strong advice: DON'T! Each person is unique with different talents and capabilities; when you start to compete and compare this can block your individual progress. It happens everywhere. People actually destroy themselves through anger, jealousy, hatred and rivalry, all triggered by comparison and competition. It is really sad that time and again people become victim of that tendency. Spiritual practice absolutely rejects this tendency. However, there is nothing wrong in getting inspired by someone who has achieved something you are aspiring towards. In any event, focus on your own progress and self-understanding.

The small anecdote of the mathematician's puzzle serves to illustrate this point:

The class was in progress, yet the boys' spirits were dull. To stimulate his pupils' minds into some activity the sensitive young teacher decided to give them a puzzle. Drawing a straight line on the blackboard, he challenged the boys to make this line appear smaller without rubbing any of it away. More than that, he announced that the one who could solve the puzzle would learn a valuable lesson for life.

Now the boys were awake. Staring at the blackboard with its solitary straight line they were truly puzzled: "How can anything be made smaller or shorter without taking away from it? It does not seem possible... maybe it is some kind of trick? Thus they pondered until at last one boy rose. The smile of understanding on his face he picked up the chalk and with a sure hand he quickly drew another, longer line next to the original one, immediately reducing the appearance of the first line. The boy's eyes shone as he looked as his teacher who had imparted such wisdom and guidance; he had truly learned a lesson for life.

Later this young mathematician was to become known as Svami Ramathirth, one of the most profound and

Enlightened Beings. And the lesson of the teacher's puzzle? Instead of demeaning another, raise yourself!

Few realize that the tendency to degrade and demean another in order to promote one's own image does more harm to oneself than to the intended victim. There is an all too common habit to humiliate a neighbor, friend or rival. The media enables millions to witness widespread propaganda aimed at exposing and undermining a competitor. Demeaning another profits no one, whereas the effort to raise oneself and one's qualities enriches all.

Mahatma Gandhi voiced a thought on this issue: "It has always been a mystery to me how men can feel themselves honored by the humiliation of their fellow beings."

Even within the 'body politics' all organs and senses are unique; all play an important role and have their own place. You cannot compare and consider one more important than the other.

There is also a small tale that highlights this principle:

One day all the organs of the body were so angry at the tummy that they went on strike. This is how it happened:

The hands complained bitterly: "Look at us; we are working our fingers to the very bone just to satisfy the tummy. We have to cook and feed the stomach all the time and it does not do any work at all."

"Yes", the eyes said, "we constantly have to go looking for food, pandering to that stomach's likes and dislikes."

The teeth also agreed: "We have to keep busy chewing, chewing, chewing and that lazy tummy does naught. All of us are working so hard except that tummy. It does absolutely nothing, just takes it all in. Hey everyone, let's go on strike and teach that tummy a lesson."

So they all stopped doing their usual tasks. There was no food for one day, two days, many days, no nourishment at all for a long time. Eventually all the complaining organs became weak, their belligerent voices less strident and lastly they went silent and reflected on their situation. It was not easy for the organs to admit that without supplying the much maligned tummy with food, they received no nourishment either and could no longer function.

At long last all the organs realized that the tummy, the whole digestive system, does the most important job of all by nourishing each and every other organ of the body. They had learned a valuable lesson. They called off the strike!

Try to remember this: On the spiritual path you cannot compare or compete. All of you have equal importance. Om Shanti.

* Also refer to: "Agni, the Sacred Fire", Chapter 8.

Chapter

2 Developing a Positive Mind

A bhajan is a type of devotional song in Indian culture. Essentially bhajans are expressions of a simple, yet profound and lyrical love for the Divine. The musical accompaniment is mostly based on classical ragas (a series of five or more musical notes upon which a melody is made - typical of Indian classical music). Bhajans have profound meaning and purpose. They have a special role in spiritual life, especially in India. They can also be performed as a kind of therapy.

Raga and ragini are played at different times of the day and on different occasions. Many North Indian ragas are performed a particular time of day or season. When performed at the stipulated time, the raga has its maximum effect.

The following bhajan is a an example of the emotions expressed by one "whose eyes have been opened"

How lucky I am
To have the audience of my true Master
He has opened my eyes, and
No longer blinded by the veil of ignorance
I am now able to see the true light
By the grace of the true Guru.

How fortunate I am
That my eyes have been opened
That I can listen to His knowledge
That no longer deluded
By the veil of illusion,
I awakened at the right time.

Safe from misery and eternal suffering
I am now guided
By the true light
Of my one and only true Guru.
How fortunate indeed I am
To have awakened at the right time.

The above bhajan represents an awakening, a realization of spiritual knowledge after a long time of patient sadhana, of spiritual practice. It is reminiscent of the Tithiri-bird who waits all year for the rain to come. It sits on a tree branch, just looking at the sky, waiting for the clouds to come - waiting for rain. Then, when first the raindrop enters its beak, it is also the time to procreate and finally its patience and longing are rewarded. This little bird serves as an example, it does not get fed up, instead it waits day in day out.

Similarly the bhajan "My eyes are opened to meet my Beloved" can become a means of meditation. The musical mystics Haridas and Surdas both used music to render spiritual bhajans. There is a legend that tells of the blind seer Surdas getting lost while walking in the forest when suddenly he felt someone taking his hand and guiding him. He knew that it was someone extraordinary and realized it could only be Krishna. This experience and others prompted him to create many devotional poems and songs.

Devotion, true love of the heart, is a very powerful element. It is not just emotional, but also physical, it affects the physical body. Most people do not realize what lies inside the physical shell, how amazingly the whole body has been structured. For those who really understand the body, the great miracle is apparent. Just think of the multiple combinations of electrons, the combinations of rays in the body and so much more. For most people the body may appear simple, yet it is profoundly complex. For example, the heart has so many physical as well as emotional manifestations. It has a corresponding energy center, the heart chakra.

Life is like a never-ending story you can immerse yourself into, yet never come to the end. Diving into your Self toward the end of life you may feel that someone is hiding the mystery from you and you wonder what life is all about. When you are young you can say: "Life is ahead of me and I will find out." However, then you get busy with all the delights and all the problems of external life and finally you find that time has slipped away and you have not been able to find out.

The Puranas describe how Brahma created himself without parents inside a lotus at the beginning of the universe, the flower emerging from the navel of Vishnu. Evidently, sitting on the lotus, he wanted to discover his roots, from where he would 'travel' to find his origin. Finally, after much traveling he heard a voice telling him that he would not find his roots through traveling; instead, the knowledge would be revealed to him through meditation on his inner Self. Brahma went into meditation.

This legend illustrates the importance of the navel chakra. It is the connection with your source, your 'mother' and through the mother's cord you receive all nourishment. If the cord is disconnected, you are disconnected.

The philosophy of the Divine Mother plays an important role in understanding the connection to our own spirituality. Spiritually and symbolically, the idea is to connect yourself to your Divine Cosmic Mother. Kali, one of the manifestations of the Divine Mother has become well known in recent years for her more destructive appearance. That kind of extreme energy represents all the forces within you. How you handle and apply those energies depends entirely on you. By way of example, fire can maintain you - you can cook, you can warm yourself - but it can equally burn you. Try to be aware that it can nurture you as well as destroy you. You need to know how to utilize those forces. The Ayurvedic principle jathagni represents the fire element in the body. On the one hand it helps you to digest food and absorb its nutrients. On the other hand, when disturbed by wrong food or constant over-feeding, there will be an overload of jathagni, resulting in indigestion and other digestive upsets. Don't burden jathagni. You are supposed to eat slowly, in small quantities, thereby giving jathagni the opportunity to do its job.

In order to become acquainted with – and understand – the physical body, you also have to understand the different aspects of your mind: In the Vedic tradition there are five kinds of mind, one main mind and 4 sub-minds :

1. manome - mind;
2. praname -understanding prana
3. aname- dealing with nourishment;
4. anandame - bliss; and
5. jnaname - dealing with knowledge

It is important to become familiar with and understand each aspect. The main life energy is prana, the life force. Everything is connected with breathing and your life energy. Pranayama takes place constantly, in everything and in the smallest action of your body. Since pranayama is so involved and complex, yet you do not notice how much pranayama is used. However, all is coordinating, constantly calibrating, re-calibrating and working together in perfect rhythm. You can help yourself by performing pranayama in combination with exercise.

Each physical manifestation of any of the five minds is very interesting. Take jnana for instance, which can assist you in understanding and translating the body language of another person. Body language can reveal a person's thoughts more clearly than words. Actually, sometimes it is good to go into silence and communicate with hand gestures. Silence can be a powerful message; it is also a good disciplinary practice from time to time. You could ask a partner to go into silence with you and observe how you can communicate. This may be difficult for some, but doing what is difficult is a matter of discipline. Training the mind to accept what is most difficult will be most helpful to your development. You should do what is very difficult for you, but of course the concept of a difficult task varies from one individual to another. Once you can accept what is difficult, it will cease to be a hardship for you.

There are countless examples of such challenges: sitting at the banks of a river, or in the wilderness at night to overcome fear; climbing a high mountain; walking alone through a dense forest, swimming in a lake when you are afraid of water; facing an animal you fear; dealing with any danger that might present itself; anything and any situation that is perceived as fearful or hardship. If you can face it, it will no longer trouble you.

The real problem is your own phobia and fear which you alone have created and carefully nurtured. Fear is not created by outside forces; fear is created only by you. This is the cause that has created suffering and pain for you. However, when you come out of your own fears and move forward, you will be free of those bonds, wherever you are. Since mind has created your phobias, it can also help you to clear them. You have to become spiritually strong and then nothing will matter to you.

It is interesting to observe how the mind works with its ego and all its emotions. Sometimes the workings of the mind may seem unclear, but when you understand how it works, the message becomes clear. The question is: do you want to be in control of yourself or do you want to be controlled by your desire, your ego, your wishes and the innumerable emotional facets of your mind?

For instance, if when provoked you do not react, it means you are not involving your ego. By not reacting, you are examining your own mind. What is your condition? Are you in control of your senses or do they rule you? Many people cannot control their emotions which resemble a team of wild horses: there is no telling where they may take you.

Therefore, if you can give feedback to your emotions by reasoning, like: 'shall I react or not react'? Then you can make your own decision. Such are the peculiarities of the human mind and they can be managed, when you make an effort to resist the triggers. You do not really know how emotions work, they can run wild, and later, when you return to sanity, you wonder why you did this or that, especially if your outburst had no meaning or reason whatsoever.

Such is the emotional mind. You do not know how the emotional mind works, how it differs during and after a crisis. You have the tendency to react to sudden situations. Only Masters, Teachers and Enlightened High Beings never do anything that does not have meaning. They do not react; everything they say and do has meaning and is never done on impulse, unlike the response of the ordinary human being who reacts according to prevailing circumstances.

That is why Satsang is important. Satsang represents an association with beings who contribute in your growth. This does not mean that you gather to sing devotional bhajans and later you quarrel. The whole idea is upliftment, of yourself and of others. But you can only do this if you have the inner strength to uplift: it cannot be done if you are weak. With strength of mind and of soul you can do anything. But if you do not have the kind of loving energy, how can you spread a positive vibration? Consider the analogy of a fan: it will distribute the prevailing air in the room. If the air is hot, it will distribute hot air, not provide cooling.

You need to understand yourself before considering another. However, it is not easy to understand yourself due to the human habit of justifying all thoughts and actions all of the time. The problem is that as long as you justify, you have no understanding and justification has become a habit. When you understand yourself it is easy to understand another; only then you can deal with anyone under any circumstances.

Sometimes things are very simple, before ego confuses the situation. Understanding yourself is the key. Then you will have no problem.

Chapter

3

Traps of Illusion

A popular Indian bhajan – devotional song – says: "Maya is a great cheat; she has been deceiving me for years. But now I know her and I am not going to get caught; I am not tempted by her various masks."

In the Bhagavad Gita Krishna says: "My maya is intriguing and full of mysteries. She has three generals, the three gunas. She is most difficult to overcome, most difficult to survive. Only those who look to ME alone will escape her net."

What is Krishna telling his disciple Arjuna? He explains that maya is actually working through you. Her gunas are aspects of all creation. In fact, creation could not have taken place without these three subtle qualities:

- Sattva - the quality of light and positivity;
- Rajas - the driving force for passion and activity; and
- Tamas - the signature of darkness, inertia and negativity.

These three qualities are maya's media of manifestation. They rotate in twenty-four hours, in a year, in a lifetime and reflect the moods of the average human being. Only one who has gone beyond, who has attained mastery over illusion, is no longer subject to the influences of these subtle qualities. Maya can only play with the weak.

Most people do not really understand maya. You are unaware of her system, and therefore you are subject to her illusion. Most people have an unclear picture of life and of themselves. Many minds do not want to believe what has not personally been experienced. It is so much easier to take a negative stance than to make the effort of examining the subject in question. You depend so much on external proofs for validation, that often you can only accept the external, material as something 'real'. This is where you encounter difficulties in growing beyond what has previously been accepted. You become trapped in illusion, cannot see how you are creating your own predicament. You may imagine things that do not exist; you think, doubt, fear, blame, hate or love - all for just nothing! In the end you find that life is empty. That is the real tragedy.

However, if you really want to bring positive change into your lives, it can be done. Through study and analysis, through discrimination, contemplation and meditation, wisdom may dawn. You may begin to see who you really are. I cannot say this too often. You need to see that you are not just body or mind, you are not ego and emotion and you have no need to identify with the qualities of ego and emotion.

It has been said before, that maya's traps do not disappear as you become more evolved. Until the final summit is reached, the chance to fall is always around the next bend. You can grow so much that you think you are better than others: this thought alone indicates that you have not grown so much after all. Anyone truly enlightened becomes more humble, like a great tree, laden with fruit, bows closer to the earth.

A long time ago in India, a philosopher watched a woman grinding wheat. He became thoughtful as he watched the grain being crushed under the big wheel - it had no chance - and he began to cry as he considered the fate of all beings, crushed and ground by the Wheel of Life, inexorably, mercilessly Kabir, the poet saint, had a son who also stood watching the grinding of the wheat. He started to laugh, When the woman asked the cause of his merriment, he replied that although most of the grain was being ground to dust, nothing happened to those kernels that took refuge in the center. He was laughing for them.

It is like the circle of maya. Those who go to the center, who return to their true origin, escape the fate of the others. As the wheel of life rotates, every human being is caught in the cycle of birth, death and suffering. This can seem cruel and discouraging, but it is possible to escape: by taking refuge in higher laws.

Chapter

4

Laws of Nature and Laws of Men

It is sad that there is a tendency to forget the wonderful bounties Mother Nature has given to us. The elements of nature contain powerful and life-giving energy which is within us and around us. The majority of man-made laws are contrary to the laws of nature throughout the world and most individual practices therefore are equally contrary to the laws of nature. When the individual practices of the laws of men are not aligned with the laws of nature then anything designed by men will fail. Man has to align his practices according to the forces of Nature.

Ultimately natural forces will always prevail. We have mentioned that some people in the USA, concerned about political trends, have tried to establish a "Natural Law Party". It may not be easy to overcome stereotypical thinking, but when all man-made laws are aligned according to the laws of nature, then things will work very much better on Planet Earth. When you develop a childlike attitude to the natural forces, Mother Nature will take good care of you.

There is a story of Kali, the personification of the most destructive energy of Mother Nature. Kali also represents the highest form of transformation, the Absolute Itself. She received her name because she devours kala (time).

The tale goes that at a time when the world was threatened by overwhelming negativities and the abuse of Mother Nature - in the form of demons - Siva had had enough and he asked his wife Parvati to destroy the demons to save the world. Thus Parvati transformed herself into Kali, ferocious in appearance and unleashed her terrible anger on the demons until there were none left. Kali's anger was so intense and she became so intoxicated by her aroused fury that the entire humanity was in danger of being destroyed. Something had to be done. Several High Beings decided to approach Lord Siva to deal with Kali's anger, pleading: "We cannot manage the anger of Kali, we request you to contain Kali's forces." Lord Siva was also concerned, thinking her anger was so much more powerful that she may not even recognize her Lord in her state as Kali. He decided to lie himself down in the path of Kali - and as she was passing, she stepped on her Lord Siva. Startled and looking down, she recognized Siva, her anger evaporated and she became Parvati again.

It would be prudent to heed the analogy: when you become infused with a childlike attitude of complete innocence and trust you are protected, but when you are ruled by ego, you will be destroyed. It is ego itself that destroys you. There is no one who has survived with a prominent ego. Look at history; especially look at the so-called "mighty and powerful".

A book has been written called "Untergang" (Downfall) that focuses on the last days of Hitler. He had changed history yet the book illustrates the complete disintegration of Hitler in mind, body and soul. It shows how helpless he became in the end when he could see no way out but to instruct his companions to take his life. There was no option left for him. In the end he was totally helpless. It was the same with Napoleon - left on St. Helena, unable to help himself, the only pleasure he had was to play with the children of his Guard. There are countless examples, in history as well as in the present, of the destructive force of individual ego gone rampant.

To rephrase: before the power of natural forces all creatures are nothing, yet especially when the human ego feeds you with thoughts that you are powerful, beautiful, smart, and so on, endowing you with countless wonderful attributes which are nothing but a veil. That veil will keep you locked in illusion. Ego will tempt you with the appearance of countless characteristics that might appeal to you.

On the spiritual path there is only one thing you can give to your Master and that is your ego - you give your ego by being humble and He/She will free you from your ego. As long as you are the victim of your own ego, you will get nowhere. In fact, you are getting progressively weaker as time goes by. Then the thought enters: I used to be so strong, whatever happened?

At one time you may have been able to "kick" people, to assert yourself, but now one kick can knock you down. This is the effect of time: once you were powerful and now you are weak. However if you have prudently gathered the spiritual force, you will always be strong. Spiritual force does not diminish and will maintain your strength.

Those involved in the performance of arts for instance have a tendency to worry about age; they live in constant fear of ageing, particularly in the western society which only admires the slim, the young and the beautiful.

Many governments would prefer you to be "gone" after retirement when you are no longer productive in the job market. Then they could avoid having to pay the pension. It seems that no one really wants the retirees. This is cruel, but it is the reality of the world we live in. You need to be aware of that, and this is why you have to develop your own strength. You need spiritual strength; you need to recognize the true energy within you, the true light and the true life. Your true life, the force within you, is the Ultimate Force. That force is part of you. You have both light and dark forces within you; you have both shadow and light, a light side and a dark side. That duality is within you and part of you. But it is up to you to decide which one you choose. Both sides are powerful. The power of light is the real power, whereas the dark side is always the destructive side. Once you can recognize the natural forces within you, you will also appreciate nature as part of you, integrated within you.

Chapter

5 Tools for Growth: Training Your Senses

Many people have lost the art of real listening, yet the spiritual path recognizes the importance of silence and the value and meaning of sound.

For instance, try to listen to the sounds in your surroundings: birds, bees, dogs, human voices, engines running; listen to them all together, like a huge environmental symphony. Then try to separate each sound from the others and listen to one sound at the time only. You may wish to practice on the most obvious sound or the least intrusive sound. See the exercise below.

Consider the example of the blacksmith, who sharpens his tools to perfection, thereby rendering them more effective. Similarly, you need to sharpen the tools of your senses, your faculties, including all the senses – vision, hearing, touch, taste, smell, feeling, etc, – so you can achieve the maximum benefit of all your senses.

For this purpose we can use a different method or technique of meditation, like concentrating on the surrounding sounds; one sound is more dominant than the other. You can focus on one less dominant - like the hum of a bee or fly or a whispering breeze, then try to tune out and block all the other sounds, Listen to each sound separately, as far as possible. Consider listening to a concert in a concert hall where you can focus on a particular instrument with the help of your eyes to hear the different instruments. You can also center your hearing on the flute or violin. Separate out one sound and listen to that, even when listening to a recorded version. You can enlist the aid of a second sense - vision - to fully appreciate what you are hearing. That is yogic meditation: to concentrate on one sound only and nothing else.

If you have five people talking, make an effort to listen to one person alone. When you have that kind of concentration then you are progressing in your meditation.

It is also very helpful to try and listen to your inner sound. There are many internal sounds within yourself, like water flowing, a whistle blowing, or a train going, even a motor sound. There are many sounds and activities within you that you are not aware of. In fact during sleep even more activities occur because the body is not disturbed. It would be an interesting experiment to record all your body's activities during sleep. It is surprising how active the body is; you could compare its activities to the sounds and activities of the night. The 15th century mystic poet Kabir states: "Inside you is the sound of your Beloved, the perennial, eternal sound, the sound of your soul. When you can hear the celestial sound you will have a vision of your Beloved. This sound will lead you to a different dimension."

Visualization is a very powerful tool; you should visualize all that is pleasant to you, especially when in surroundings that can be disturbing like in a crowded train or bus, at the railway station, or in a waiting room. That is the time to bring in the memory of your own pleasant impressions and block out all the unpleasant and disturbing sounds and images. This will allow you not to suffer in a crowd, but rather select your own theme and visualization. In fact, when you go to sleep you can implant into your subconscious the kind of dream you like to have; you can program what you want to dream, then, when in deep sleep, the intent will manifest in your dream. That is one technique to choose what you want to dream.

You can have day dreams and nightmares; the latter unfolds when you have a disturbed mind or have some interference in your body, like drugs or alcohol. The beautiful dreams you can program into your subconscious resemble the process of burning your images and impressions onto a CD.

There are some classical programs on the radio - so pleasant to listen to that it is like sliding into a different stage - but then a rough awakening comes with loud and disturbing advertising offering you the finest tomato soup. This can actually be a considerable a shock to the system. What can you do? These are the daily commercials we cannot seem to escape.

On the old radios you had the tuning dial to carefully achieve the best reception of your selected program. This is a fitting analogy for learning to finely tune your mind's dial to concentrate on each of your senses individually so you can reject all disturbing sounds around you. You may want to go into the beautiful countryside to try your senses and when you can fine-tune to your senses you will see improvement in your life.

This also assists in discrimination of anything that is offered to you, food for example: you will be able to discriminate if the food is pure and fresh or stale and filled with chemicals.

When you can fine-tune your faculties like that you will be gaining more joy from your senses with maximum satisfaction of each act. You could say that this is the antidote to the distractions of modern living - of doing several things together, yet not doing anything properly. Each act done with full attention becomes a meditation, and when you make each act into a meditation, you will be enlightened. Each act is sadhana and tapasya - spiritual practice and penance - and becomes meaningful as such. Accordingly you do not need to do morning and evening meditation; instead meditation has become an integrated part of your life.

A Vedic Mantra states: "Whatever I do, whatever I say, whatever I think, eat, perform, may all acts of mine become meaningful. Every act of mine should become puja."

Thus every act becomes divine, such as offering of fruit, flower or anything that is offered with devotion and dedication. Take this example: whenever you invite someone whom you like, you prepare your home for the guest. The person who does the preparation has often greater pleasure than the guest. The person who is performing the preparation has the satisfaction of offering; a sense of fulfillment so great that this act gives instant happiness. Looking at the flowers, the food, the painting, the arrangement, it all together brings a great sense of pleasure.

However, it can be very disappointing if the guest remarks that the tea is too weak or too strong, the cake is too sweet or not sweet enough, the flowers give him allergies - happiness can disappear. It all depends on the kind of guest you invite. Who you invite is in your hands and requires positive discrimination. You are responsible, you create the momentum and the intensity and the other person should complement the situation. The sense of discrimination represents another important tool on the spiritual path. The Sun may be there but you can only feel its warmth if you have the perception of sunshine. When you associate with those in the divine circle, this should reflect in your life and lead you to the excellence reflected by the Divine.

In the words of a yogic prayer: "Let my sleep become a samadhi, every act I do, when I speak, should be an offering and praise to the Lord."

Chapter

6 Listening to the Inner Self

Listening to your inner Self from time to time is very important. Many have a habit of keeping the mind engaged and busy with outer things and activities. However, it is when you are in silence that you can attune to the nature around you. When you have nothing else to do externally, then you are "bored" - there is nothing to keep your mind occupied with outer activities. You can repeat countless external acts. From morning to night you are either looking after your body, you are eating, talking and doing all kinds of other busy work, and you are totally immersed in externals.

Whenever there is inactivity of body you get concerned about keeping the mind busy. Yet the mind is always busy, even during sleep and when dreaming; mind is always working, never rests, always doing something. That is its function. Actually, it is a cultural habit to think that you are not doing anything, although a lot is going on within you. When you are not busy with externals, why not try to attune to your inner world, your inner aspects? You can connect to your mind, to your emotions and even your body's organs, to your chakras and of course to your Self. These things never rest. That is why people find it difficult to be in silence. More than that; often silence is even perceived as punishment. Silence is the state where you can gather energy - where you recharge your human battery! In fact, when you are talking, you lose energy, especially when you talk nonsense. It is like eating chocolate or ice cream; if you examine the nutrition you will find it wanting.

When you talk meaninglessly, letting your tongue loose, it is merely entertainment. Compare this to spices which make the food delicious, but have little or no nutritional value.

When we speak we do not always mean what we say. Politicians have made it a skill to say something that may have a very different meaning. If some expert would "translate" what politicians say, for instance "I want to serve..."; this is likely to mean "I want to improve my position". Almost all politicians do that - they say something, yet mean something else.

When you go into silence during meditation - listening to yourself as you are - you connect to your true Self. In silence everything is transparent, in silence you have no fear, and there is no fear of duality. It is only if you consider someone separate from you, maybe some stranger, someone not familiar, not connected or attuned to you, then you create fear. This presents a wall that separates you from another being. Look at children, how fearless they are. They have no conditioning; that comes later and is the result of learned thinking. Then all the conditioning through parents and surroundings takes over and a wall is created. It becomes like a dark curtain that you cannot see through; a curtain of ignorance, of simply not knowing. When you do not know, you create fear, doubt and hostility and finally hate. It becomes a situation where all the negative forces will congregate.

Separation from others will create fear and anxiety, whereas oneness will create love, affection and understanding. When you are in silence, you have the opportunity to experience oneness with your Self and all other aspects of your interactions. In silence things are transparent.

Silence, however, is also a force, an energy which can be difficult to endure and tolerate. You are scared of your own Self, your own force. You may not always want to know this, but the interesting aspect is that it gives you the opportunity of facing who and what you are, even though you would rather run away from yourself. Almost all genuine spiritual therapies focus on silence.

It is not uncommon in India for a Sadhu, a wandering seeker of the truth, to go to unusual means of overcoming fear and facing the reality of oneself. Indeed, one Sadhu was known to visit the crematoria in silence to overcome fear in general - and especially the fear of death - by facing the reality of the impermanent physical body.

When you have the realization of various aspects of your life, when you can see yourself and observe what kind of state you are in, you will come to know the many different states of mind. Each different state of mind, each level of consciousness, will bring different emotions. In twenty-four hours you are going through a host of different emotional states; you can experience the highs of positively concentrated energy of mind as well as being subjected to the mind's lows. But if you can learn to harness the energy of yourself you will be able to utilize this force for maintaining yourself in perfect health and balance.

Currently humanity is facing a challenge to harness the natural energy surrounding us rather than relying on centuries old fossil fuel energy. Similarly we have a lot of energy within us that we can use to heal and recharge ourselves. Unfortunately the problem is that we do not know how to find the right attitude, how to achieve this, but the solution definitely exists. Take the example of learning computer skills or using a cell phone or digital camera. Unless you understand how to do it, the technology is meaningless to you. In the same vein, unless you know how to harness your own energy, you cannot know how to rejuvenate or how to address any deficiencies of nutritional aspects.

Find the solution for the problem you are facing and remove the targeted deficiency. For instance if there is a deficiency of Vitamin C, your resistance will be low, your immune system weak and you may be prone to infection.

You know that you can remove the deficiency from your system by adding Vitamin C to your food intake.

Your deficiency may be physical or emotional : you need to deal with it and all will be well. Remember the days when television and technology first made their appearance. It was quite exciting. Many thought that they no longer needed human company. Initially this was the case, but then people realized that TV cannot compensate for interaction with real people. You cannot ask anything, cannot have a discussion, in short, it was not the answer for your life. Then computers were developed where you can ask questions and have some interaction. Could this be the new companion to make you happy? You can send and receive mail and you can talk to others on the computer, even see their faces while talking. Alright, you might think, I have found the ideal companion. Then you realize that, even with all these capabilities, finally the computer is not the perfect solution either. It can help you, yes, but a computer cannot compensate for real human contact. There simply is no compensation. It is back to basics; you have tried all the modern technology and finally you have come back to basics. First you run away from each other and yourself, then you want each other back.

How are you to find the balance? You need balanced communication - you need a sense of balance and happiness which is mutually complementing. The great Mystic Tulsidas said: "There are two types of individuals in my life and both are cruel to me - those that come into my life and others who are leaving my life. Both make me upset."

Sometimes one careless remark can make you very angry, especially when people allow their tongues to run wild and out of control. Speech can be the most dangerous and poisonous tool if not used rightly. It is not easy to find a balanced human being, whose association enriches you. It comes back to the point of facing yourself, looking at your own mistakes, examining your own shortcomings. Compare this to weeds growing in your flowers and grass. How can you eliminate the weeds? Take a look at what your priorities are in your life. Many times I see that people have very wrong priorities. Do you ask yourself what makes you happy and fulfilled? What helps you to learn and grow, to evolve and inspire? And what makes you unhappy and miserable? Many seem to follow a path that constantly makes them miserable. It is a strange dilemma which requires a positive change. I inspire people to have satsang, to get together periodically to inspire each other and to evolve along their paths.

It is also interesting to see that people actually long to have positive environment where they can grow and be happy, yet often proceed to destroy this very environment by contradictory behavior. The whole idea is to inspire and help themselves and each other and create a mutually nurturing environment. That kind of environment can create evolution which is the whole concept of life. If you look at the entire cosmos and nature, you will see that everything is evolving, including individuals. You want beauty, peace and happiness, and when opportunity presents itself, it is a good idea to bring it to fruition.

At present the power of money has become the most important focus in the world. Money has become the goal; other aspects are being ignored. Throughout the world there are many construction projects going on, without consideration for the environment and for the social and spiritual concerns. There is no longer any balance: balance has been lost to the power of materialism which has obscured the fact that other aspects are also very important.

You need to think carefully what makes your life happy and fulfilling, individually and as a group. It is important that you promote those qualities and positive aspects of life. In general it seems that people often want to follow the spiritual path, yet they cannot sustain it. Spiritual awareness is vital to our survival and we have to work toward that and make people see how important it is not to follow blindly "what everyone is doing".

If you lose balance, you lose everything. It seems that the power of materialism is so strong that you can get lost. It is like an infection of modern life. To withstand this influence and bring balance back into your life is an individual pursuit; one has to be aware of one's thought, speech and actions. There is no reason not to enjoy such time which is of benefit to your entire being. It is a time to celebrate life and to experience all you are longing for. By listening to your Inner Self you have this opportunity, enjoy it to the fullest and make the most of it.

Chapter

7

Layers of Love

Many of you have questions about love. Love is a complex and vast subject of many different levels and many different layers. Much is determined by your individual understanding, your experiences and how you have learned to deal with its ramifications.

Let us explore some of these layers: we can talk about basic love, elevated love and finally divine love. This may seem like complicated terminology but love is not easily defined. It depends on which layer you are dealing with at a given time.

Consider love versus expectation. For the average person feeling love, there are also expectations and expectations can bring much suffering when those expectations are not being met. Very simply, when you do not expect, you do not become disappointed. Therefore, the safest form of love is that which has no expectation of reward or reciprocation. Thus you can avoid a lot of pain and suffering. It may not be easy to practice love without expectation, but it is well worth the effort.

However, there can also be side effects, when you feel that you are being taken for granted. You may do so much that you become totally exhausted and still there is no recognition for the labors of your love. For a love to be fulfilling, it has to be mutually rewarding.

When others appreciate your love, it is reciprocally satisfying, but if you are being taken for a ride, then you may begin to wonder. What can you do if the relationship is totally one-sided? You need to have a dialogue; you need to express what you feel. It can happen that the other person may not even be aware of your feelings and does not understand. You have to speak your mind, express your feelings. Communication is essential.

Another situation can occur with persons, deprived of love through life's harsh circumstances; they will actually appreciate any offerings of love much more.

There are also situations where you can become swamped by love and that can be equally hard to handle. In some cases it can even become a burden, a feeling of being suffocated. Again, communication is the key.

And then there is conditional love, one of the most treacherous forms, especially when geared toward children. A child growing up with enticements like "if you do this I will love you, otherwise not" may grow up never feeling appreciated and safe in any relationship unless he or she can proffer something first.

People have different understanding and definition of what constitutes love in their minds. Unfortunately, when they do not discuss, misunderstandings multiply, finally resulting in a complete breakdown of communication and break-up of the relationship. All this pain and upset, because nothing was discussed! Communication is vital to define the layer of love you are involved in. If you identify your meaning and your understanding of love and its expectation, this is a much safer start.

The term 'love' is often used so casually that it can lose its profound meaning. No doubt, love is intricate and commonly used with both highest and lowest energy. It is the most complex, most intriguing, most mysterious and mystical emotion, yet we cannot do without love. It is the paramount force. If you really feel that no one loves you, that mirrors a state of disaster.

Then there is another and very different love: the love of the true Sat Guru. Of course, the love of the Sat Guru is poles apart; it is based on knowledge and never based on give and take. There is no 'deal' in a purely spiritual relationship. Since spiritual growth has no end, the relationship with the Sat Guru can last forever - life after life. This connection, this bond is never based on appearance, never on age or gender. This association is based only on a pure and spiritual foundation.

In contrast, worldly love is as diverse as the various cultures, upbringings and environments. Consider the love for a child: any transgression or mistake by the child does not make you very angry; you know that the child has a different understanding, is still learning, and so you forgive. But dealing with love in a partnership can bring a lot of anger, again, due to expectations. The higher the expectations, the greater the anger. As I have said before: try to have minimal expectations and your love can blossom much more.

Love is so mysterious : it keeps on flowing and you cannot really pinpoint the different layers of love. Yet if love is based on communication, you have found the sustainer and purifier of love. However, if you love someone and you do not feel any reciprocation, love will deteriorate and finally die. The main challenges in any relationship are desire, want and the ever-present ego. I always advise people: "if you cannot uplift yourself, don't lower yourself." There are times and situations when you may feel so bad, so disappointed, and so very angry that you want to retaliate, lash out and be hurtful. This serves no one, neither the angry person, nor the person upon whom this fury is focused. It lowers everyone and can become cyclical.

There are people who do not want to communicate due to a variety of reasons and 'hang-ups'. Some have problems or may feel inhibited by fear of not being able to handle communication. Others may find it difficult to discuss, define or verbalize emotions. However it is the result of the emotions which is the real substance and that you can discuss.

The prime example is jealousy. Jealous people do all kind of outrageous things based on their own insecurity. It is a very common disease. Whatever happens, it should be discussed. If it is ignored, the other person may get very worked up and if the situation is not handled carefully, it can become explosive, even violent. It is so much better and easier for everyone to make an effort to diffuse the situation rather than react and increase the negative energy with the potential of violence. Do not harbor negative feelings. I always try to resolve any conflict and move on, both for the sake of myself as well as for the sake of the other person. If you accumulate harmful feelings, you will suffer. It is like freshly fallen snow, which is easy to clear when new, but if your leave it, it becomes a hard and icy snow-pack which is very difficult to shift. Try to release any negatives as you go. This does not mean that you do not care, but the obstacle has to be removed. For sooner or later it could escalate. It does not have to come to that. Problems will always manifest, they are a part of life; your job is to resolve them.

Others again do not want to hear the word 'love'; they are fearful of their own vulnerabilities and have become experts in building a wall around their emotions. Sooner or later they will have to break that wall.

Misuse of the term love is common both in politics and in religion. There is an old song from the Second World War, exclaiming in its lyrics: "Praise the Lord and pass the ammunition" that gives a glimpse of the misuse of love. It is easy to misuse the term for something else and far removed from its essence, in religion as well as in politics. Whether in groups or individuals, the expression 'love' is often used for individual or collective gain and manipulation. People regularly use powerful terms and expressions of love to inspire support for groups and individual causes to get what they want, whereas in fact there is no feeling of love whatsoever. Love is a powerful term with impact.

When you analyze the contents of the Ten Commandments you will see that they are based on practical common sense, socially- structured laws. It is common sense that when you live together you do not disturb the social environment. People refer to God to gain maximum impact; yet, if you examine, it is clear that you should not want to disturb your community or neighbor. At the same time, dispute with a neighbor is very common throughout the world. If a law had to be established as a divine rule, this only demonstrates the consciousness of Kali Yuga. Of course you should be able to get on with everyone. You may use the term 'love' but to love everyone is neither really feasible nor realistic.

By way of example, consider the countless religious wars, spanning many centuries. In the scenario of emotionally charged people, look at the conflict between religions throughout history, each faction proclaiming to be right, with swords, guns and whatever devastating weapon the human mind can create. How can you hope to love everyone? It is not possible. The appropriate term is to tolerate your neighbor. If humanity can achieve tolerance that would be a major achievement. The real problem is that people do not tolerate and therefore destroy.

How can you communicate with people who are locked in fanaticism? This is the big question within the human race: how can you convey the message? You cannot change the religion, the culture or the fundamentals of any religion, so what can you do? Ideally there should be a worldwide debate on the role of religion. When you have a worldwide debate, then many issues of conflict can be resolved. You may not like others, but you can learn to tolerate them. It is like neutralizing the situation.

Successful debate also begins with individual love. When you start loving and discovering yourself, realizing the potential, the understanding, the feeling and many other beautiful aspects, then you can share these discoveries with others. Just as when a child comes to you full of excitement after discovering something new and you have to participate in this excitement to assist in the child's discovery. When you learn to participate and celebrate, then collectively people can create a beautiful environment.

Always, when you interact with people, there can be a great deal of emotion. For instance, you go to your workplace day in day out, spend eight hours daily with other people around you with whom you may have nothing in common apart from the work you do. Is it not important to bring a common ground to have a good interaction with your co-workers on an objective basis? There should be no personal expectation, except in the work done well and this should result in some kind of mutual understanding and harmony.

There is a Proverb: "Look at your own space and tend your own garden".

You need to understand your role and the role of others around you. If you don't have clear role of yourself, then you can have a problem with others. Try to maintain harmony in all your circumstances with a more positive and selfless loving attitude without expectations.

Chapter

8

Agni, the Sacred Fire

In Vedic times it was customary to invoke the energies of the five great elements as the components of all living beings. These five elements: Agni (fire), Vayu(air), Prithivi(earth), Jal(water) and Akasa (space) are always present and are revered as deities. Moreover, all living beings which exist in this world have these five basic elements, from which their bodies are made.

Let us focus and meditate on Agni, fire. Fire is present at all times and everywhere - including in your body - and fire is invisible as well as visible. It is present within you and around you. Agni is considered the prime deity and the witness of a marriage ceremony. As an example, consider that during a Vedic marriage ceremony the bride and groom circle the fire seven times - symbolizing seven conditions both partners have to agree to. This solidifies the marriage as evidenced by the fact that fire cannot be influenced, unlike wind and water for instance.

Vedic people considered that through these five vital elements contact with the Supreme Being can be established. The methods of worship are completely scientific, because the rituals which are performed to worship the five deities (Panch Mahabhuta) focus on the understanding of cosmic and natural law.

. Fire is also considered to be the direct representative of the Supreme Being, of the Ultimate Reality. It is important to gain some understanding of the fire within and the fire outside you, to comprehend the role of fire and the meaning and functioning of fire in your life and beyond - an understanding that the invisible became visible due to necessity. The individual fire has always been present, just as Atma has always been present.

Whenever there is a greater need for Atma - the Self, the Immortal Soul - to manifest through you, you will discover your own atmik energy which leads to Self Realization if you make a true effort. It is a revelation of your own Self. You have been separated from your Self for a long time and returning to your Self is like coming home; it is a meeting with your True Self. When you face the fire, you are facing our own Atma, your True Self, and when that takes place, you can truly see who and what you are. Fire is a great symbol for understanding the workings of our own being, of witnessing your own Self's mystery and every aspect of life.

There is so much mystery involved in life and it is up to you to discover each mystery, one by one, to understand the purpose and role in our own life. Once you can do this, everything else will fall into place.

The celebration of fire is called a Jnana Yagna (Yagna of knowledge). It is a ceremony whereby the energy to ask for contact with High Beings is invoked, asking them to come and reveal themselves to you. This ceremony becomes a means of connecting to High Beings. In Vedic tradition fire and Yagna are used as a celebration and discovery of knowledge.

Once again you are enriched with a further layer of knowledge. The layers of knowledge can be compared to the various strata in earth layers. Each time you participate in a Jnana Yagna you add another layer of knowledge. All this becomes part of your personal wealth and it is something to treasure. It all becomes part of our consciousness. Every spoken word becomes part of the akashik records and it is lasting. When you have access to the akashik records, it depends on how you use the knowledge. Consider the accumulation of this knowledge like your own library and make use of the knowledge you have discovered. Such knowledge is not just for storage in the archives which can soon be forgotten. Nothing is lost or wasted. Then how can you make the best use of this knowledge, especially when you have a crisis in your life? You need to recollect the particular formula and apply that to your life, thereby finding the solution to resolve the problem. That is how it works, but you have to remind yourself. You may have forgotten the formula, and have to jog your memory that you do not forget the eternal truth which is the very basis of life and which is always there with you. All knowledge is available, and you ask: "How can I make the right use of this knowledge and apply its wisdom in my life? Well, in the beginning this may be challenging, but as you continue to practice, it can become part of your life. Try to keep this knowledge as alive and glowing as the fire.

Many of you have seen the orange dhoti of a sanyasin. This symbolizes the fire wherein all his worldly desires have burned. Now it is only the eternal flame of spiritual love and bliss which is burning. If you can become as vibrant as the fire — positively and with great strength and energy — it becomes a process of purification and a great symbol of life. That knowledge is as vibrant as fire and extinguishes all anxiety.

Fire is also a symbol of protection. For example, if you light a fire in the wilderness, no animal will come near you. It also gives you warmth, you can cook a meal on it, and it enhances the interaction with good company. Fire has played an important and vital role in all cultures and civilizations. Fire has been the focus of age old ceremonies, even going back to the Stone Age where the discovery of fire presented a major mile stone of evolution.

Having examined these many aspects of yourselves, having looked at another dimension of yourselves, try to maintain these memories for the benefit of yourself and others. This is another element of your life to bring fullness into your lives. You have learned that nothing is impossible, that all is part of the WHOLE, all is complete, purna. Remember the great Vedic mantra which is at the core of Vedantic teachings: Om purnamadah purnamidam purnat – nothing is incomplete, what I see and what I don't see: we are all whole. Then continue to remind yourself that you are complete; you are not 'defective'. This concept of being 'defective' somehow has crept into the human consciousness and it is wrong. The Purna Mantra is a powerful invocation and meditation. Invoke your energy, and whatever darkness may have entered your consciousness, direct the light of knowledge there while chanting the Mantra.

"om purnamadah purnamidam purnat purnamudacyate purnasya purnàmadaya purnameva vashisyate"

Chapter

9

Connecting to Your Higher Self: A Question of Power

Meditation can be done anytime and anywhere in order to connect to your higher Self and use your energy and power in a balanced manner. It is a state of mind, an attunement and a connection to yourself and your higher Self. It is a tool that can provide a connection to your senses and to your body. Most of the time your mind and all your senses are disconnected and not working in harmony. Rather they resemble wild horses running in all directions.

One of those wild horses is anger, an emotion only too common. Anger can make you lose complete control over yourself, over speech and all your actions, often leading to the kind of calamity that has far reaching results. Words you may speak in anger can do untold harm and even if you change your mind when sanity returns, the impact remains. Remember the adage "you cannot unring a bell".

Another common aspect of the wild horses is depression. It is sometimes referred to as an attack by the "wild black dog". When depression controls your mind, all around you appears in shades of gray and black. There is an absence of color and an absence of light. All is dark and obscured; you cannot see a way out. Similarly, in a dark room you cannot see; and when the mind is in darkness it is equally complex to find a solution to your current difficulties. Therefore, it is best not to make an important decision when thus handicapped by the "wild black dog" of depression.*

Depression is like an overcast sky, full of dark clouds. Consider how you feel when the sky is overcast; how it affects both your body and your mind. Even dull weather can influence your entire being with a sensation of heaviness and inertia. You are affected by so many aspects: by planets, by weather, by the vibration of your surroundings and by other people. No matter how logically and rationally you wish to analyze, there are some things you just cannot explain. You know that some days all is well and fine, when everything moves smoothly and simply clicks into place, whereas other days start poorly and all that can go wrong will go wrong. We are all familiar with both extremes.

There are many countries where people will consult an astrologer to explore the influences of the planets so they may utilize the positive influences and avoid the negative trends of some days. When the stars are in your favor important events and scheduled decisions have a better chance of a positive outcome.

However, it is spiritual power and energy which will make a difference. If you are spiritually protected, many negative influences will have little effect on you. Such protection is like a "spiritual insurance" and does not fail. But then the question arises: Have you paid your spiritual insurance premium - the premium in the form of love and trust, dedication, devotion, humility and service?

Life is not as simple as it may appear at times; in fact, it is as complex as the human mind and human emotions. This complexity becomes apparent when an unexpected event takes place. Your mind perceives something and quickly you follow your mind's dictates by some form of action or reaction, irrespective of the event being positive or negative. Rarely do you question the wisdom of your action/reaction, you just do it. You follow an impulse without examining and evaluating the situation. Sadly, people have very few positive impulses. Acting on impulse is rarely the way to resolve any situation or conflict.

Conversely, meditation is the exception, where acting on impulse is recommended. There is no time table for meditation; rather take the opportunity to use any moment that your mind is peaceful and try to drift into the state of meditation. A disturbed and restless mind makes things difficult. No matter how insignificant, small or silly the trigger, those moments of disturbed mind can make meditation impossible. The human mind does not need serious aspects to be upset; it is the consummate expert in dramatizing and multiplying a tiny disagreement into a crisis.

It takes a long time to overcome such impulses, which affect your bodily functions and your mental equilibrium; the whole body politics come into play. Rather than letting small things snowball into major effects, learn to minimize the problem and avoid a crisis, whether at home, at work, or wherever you may be. But that kind of skill and control has to come from a natural spiritual impulse; it cannot be forced or pretended. It has to become an integral part of your being, reflecting the natural sensation of "I am peaceful".

That is the natural process to resolve your crisis, the process to drift into the state of meditation. It is also good to sit together and create an atmosphere that will create relaxation. You can offer some refreshment. "Shall we have tea?" A cup of tea is always welcome, no one objects and it connects and relaxes people. You can talk to your mind and ask it: are you happy? Mind says "no", and then you ask: "why not?" "I don't have this and that". It is healthy to have a dialogue with your mind; you can convince yourself and you can be your own guru.

The relationship with your Sat Guru is spiritual. It is based on the divine nature - that is where you are related. It is intended that you tell everything to your Sat Guru in confidence to bring light to your consciousness and resolve your confusion. The Sat Guru's role is clearly defined, but you should also be your own guru, and take responsibility for yourself.

Whatever you are associated with, you take that quality upon yourself. It is like walking in a beautiful flower garden. When you come out of the garden, wherever you go you radiate that fragrance. It is not unusual that at times people want you to join in some activity that is their personal "thrill", some pursuit that is not always healthy or good for you. Then the question arises: what is the reason they want you to join? Is it to bring you down to their level? What is the real reason? Ask the other person: Is it the guilt of a personal habit that will make you less guilty if I joined you? This is just an example of the very tricky and complex workings of the human mind.

You need to become friends with your senses. Why are you depressed, angry, upset, etc? Why are you frustrated? Try to find the answer within yourself and establish happiness within yourself, each moment, here and now, not sometime in the future. I am going to be happy NOW.

When you have come to accept your own emotions in a natural way, you will recognize them as part of you and your own personality. Once you accept them as such, they become easy to manage. Remember that they are not visitors or outsiders; they are a part of you and your many manifestations! It is important to understand the varying types of energy that human beings manifest.

According to Vedic principles Shakti, power, comes in many forms. An extreme form is Kali. She is the symbol of extreme energy and we can only hope that it will not come to that. Shakti is said to have nine different forms of manifestation - each representing a different aspect of life. It is the kind of energy that is constantly expanding and contracting.

It should be easy to withdraw from outside influences and drift into meditation, out of the millions of temporary bubbles or life experiences which dissolve and reform constantly. Creation and dissolution form a continuous process of the cycles of mind and emotion. The average human being is subject to such fluctuations, but a High Being is like a power house who can create high waves out of nothing; Try to become as powerful that wherever you go you will be the one who can create positive energy.

Often, after the arrival of the Sat Guru when on the spiritual path there may be many crises, at times resembling the energy of a storm. That energy cannot be ignored and cannot be hidden. When you are growing spiritually and follow positive practices, such positive energy will evolve and be balanced.

Humans create collective perception, thinking that without ME nothing can work. That is merely the voice of ego, unless you realize that you are either everything as part of the whole, or you are nothing. Consider this: One has to recognize one's true Self to be everything. Otherwise, on the human level, a human is nothing, just a temporary being with temporary assignment and having a temporary job in this life and definitely not irreplaceable. It is a case of mistaken identity. Having lost your real identity, yet on some level you are aware of that and you continue to search, often in the wrong places. So you remain in limbo: arguing, fighting and caught in illusion, creating much suffering and pain until you realize what you have done.

In this world "I am" refers to the body as a position of power; people do not refer to the true Self with that statement. The pain, confusion and suffering based on such mistaken identity is evidenced in the dealings of many politicians, who have been empowered by the people. Collectively we empower people, then we see the ensuing disaster and we blame them. It is all about empowerment. If power is given to the wrong person this will generally result in misuse, depending on the kind of person thus endowed. If that person is decent and responsible they can use power for universal goodness. The concern today in the world is that the wrong leaders have been empowered: Power has been placed in the wrong hands. People running this world are not fit or competent. Yet the power, if not utilized, will destroy, as is evident in various global policies and conditions, such as climate change. People could destroy themselves, by changing the energy of the planet and impacting on the potential for human life, hence the significance of respecting the main elements as understood in Vedic philosophy. The Sat Guru enables such wisdom and guidance; without this humanity is much poorer.

To handle such power responsibly will need wisdom and guidance; the Sat Guru should give the wisdom, whereas if you have no Sat Guru and no guidance, it is much more difficult. To guide a nation, to rule, you need to have wisdom combined with the power.

Notes:

*The color black has many different meanings and is not always negative. Without black other colors do not exist. Black also represents the night and the dark forces within you, for instance when you are under the influence of depression.

**The generic term Shakti denotes the Universal feminine creative principle and the energizing force behind all male divinity including Shiva. Shakti is known by the general name Devi, from the root 'div', meaning to shine. She is the Shining One, who is given different names in different places and in different appearances, as the symbol of the life-giving powers of the Universe.

Chapter

10 Concept of the Sat Guru and Phases of Time

From the beginning of human existence the cycles of celestial bodies have always played a large role. Early man was necessarily attuned to the seasons as well as to the changes of day and night with its recurring phases of light and dark. Over time the cycles of Sun and Moon were used to determine time, eventually creating calendars that calculated the cycles of Sun or Moon thereby providing a concept of time. In some cultures the calendar was based on the Moon phases, later others focused on the cycles of the Sun.

The Indian calendar for instance is calculated by the Moon phases - 28 days of one cycle are divided into 2 parts - 14 days are called 'paksh' one waxing and one waning phase of the Moon.

The full Moon has a very prominent place in India; each full Moon has some spiritual significance and is always considered a positive force, unlike the traditional meaning in the Western world where werewolves and Dracula legends have given the full Moon a highly negative connotation of prevailing dark forces.

The full Moon of July/August is Guru Purnima. This is the day dedicated to the Sat Guru, the teacher, and preceptor. The term guru literally means "dispeller or remover of darkness", the one who brings light into your life, removing confusion and ignorance and bringing clarity and knowledge. Sat means the highest Truth. You need to learn to recognize the Sat Guru. However one should avoid negative influences that cause conflict.

The concept of the Sat Guru in India goes back to the beginning of time, to the time of creation.* It is a unique concept, given to the world by India. The relationship between Sat Guru and disciple is strictly spiritual and divine, not worldly, not material, quite unlike the relationship to your family and friends.

There are few things in this world which are as distinctive in the human civilization; these are aspects that should be preserved, kept closely guarded and maintained. That is the model of Sat Guru. Humans can have a collective guru as well as an individual guru, preceptor, guide, or teacher. It is a beautiful tradition and it is said that without a guru you are like a tree without fruit, a river without water, a field without crops and a garden without flowers - in other words: barren. That is the purpose and the importance of having a guru in your life. You are in this body to learn and grow! Your mother is considered your first guru; when you have evolved enough to be ready for the final guru: the Sat Guru. He guides you across the vast ocean of eternity; He is the One to take you to your ultimate destination. Yet before you are ready for this step, you must go through various "gurus'" training.

Anyone can have an ordinary guru but to find the Sat Guru is very difficult indeed. The Sat Guru will only appear when you are qualified and ready for the final steps. Otherwise you will neither recognize, nor value or benefit from him. Of course you can also "graduate" from the school of an ordinary guru and join the "University" of the Sat Guru. There is an Indian proverb that says: "Drink water only after filtering out any impurities".

In addition to the Moon phases the Indian calendar has some very definite distinctions differing from the western calendar. Vast time segments are divided into yugas as follows, for instance:

Yugas: starting with Satya Yuga - the golden age
Treta Yuga - the silver age
DvaparaYuga - the twilight age
Kali Yuga - the dark age

After the completion of one cycle there is supposed to be dissolution; however, it can happen that there is simply a slide into the next age. Imagine that one day you wake up and all is changed; people are kind to each other, there is no war, no conflict, no quarrel, no backbiting or criticism, no poverty and all are caring and sharing. No one suffers from pain or disease. In short, there is no manifestation of any form of negativity. All are happy and that would be the day of Satya Yuga. Maybe not today, but hope for it! However, when you awaken and you are being shouted at, maybe the pains of arthritis are nudging you - you will know that nothing has changed. Kali Yuga is the worst of all the ages, but importantly, even in Kali Yuga you can create your own golden age by following the spiritual path. That privilege is always given. If you follow the spiritual path, applying the teachings imparted by your spiritual Master, that exception is given. So essentially, it is in your hand to choose; you can create a golden age and the effect of Kali Yuga on you will be greatly minimized.

The Sat Guru has his own domain, His cwn territory. Kali Yuga can come in disguise and pretend to be a disciple, but comes to disturb the golden equilibrium and atmosphere, looking for a victim to derail. Sometimes Kali Yuga succeeds, but if you are aware, you do not allow the machinations of Kali Yuga to enter. Those that are affected by Kali Yuga will try to subtly attack the Sat Guru by spreading false tales and other derogatory remarks.

According to Indian tradition, the further back you go the more positive the times, whereas according to western concept the Dark Age preceded and all is supposed to be better now. This is a limited outlook since Western tradition only takes into account a few thousand years. Indian concept considers many millennia, notwithstanding various cultures' concepts of dates of civilization and time. Dating civilization is an inexact and confusing science - no one is sure.

Many spiritual Masters - such as Buddha - have chosen the full Moon as the time for annual celebration, rather than celebrating their physical birthdays. Many prefer Guru Purnima - the day of the Sat Guru (spiritual Teacher, Master or Guide) falling on the full Moon of July/August. This is the day designated for those who are committed to the teachings (often called "disciples/students") to demonstrate and renew their commitment and love toward their Sat Guru and to follow the spiritual path. It is also a day for the Sat Guru to assess the development of the disciples and the disciples to submit their commitment, as well as to evaluate how far they have come, and more importantly, how much further they have to go - as they integrate the spiritual path, awareness and practice into their lives as a whole, Key to this reflection and assessment is the concept of responsibility for self and a holistic approach to life, applying the spiritual teaching to everyday life and becoming self-sufficient while assisting fellow travelers on the path.

When teaching is imparted and knowledge is given, one is supposed to apply these principles and lessons in life. You can liken it to a given key that you are supposed to use wisely, opening the right door, not a wrong one. It is also your responsibility to use the knowledge you have been given the right way. This too requires contemplation and periodic reflection: Guru Purnima provides such an opportunity to reflect and to make positive changes in one's life.

Many people want to escape reality. This is not a solution. Rather, face the reality of your own truth. It is only by facing your truth that you can face your fear or phobia. When you actually confront your fear, your reality, you will discover that there was nothing to fear to begin with. You have built up conditioning about something you did not know and created your own phobias.

Every day in your life you make a decision. Having been given spiritual knowledge you are more able and equipped to make the right decision, a balanced decision in the sense of what brings true fulfillment to your life.

Then what is the role of the Sat Guru? This has been explained in many spiritual texts: the Guru is the remover of darkness and ignorance, leading you from untruth to truth, from darkness into light and from death to immortality (Asadoma Satagamaya) toward enlightenment. The Sat Guru gives you the key to open the right door and to make the right decisions. You should reflect upon how far your understanding has developed as a result of such experience and enjoy Guru Purnima in the spirit of positive growth and progress on the path.

There is a story which illustrates the need to observe progress along the path and the role of the Sat Guru:

A Master had been teaching a long-standing disciple the sacred lessons of the Bhagavad-Gita for several years. After all this time it was reasonable to expect that the disciple should implement the teachings in his daily life - live according to the lessons learned. And so, one fine day the Master decided to leave for a long journey.

Many years had passed when the Master decided to return and visit his disciple. As he approached the home of his disciple he noticed a lot of activity, children running back and forth and a woman's voice trying to restore some order. Eventually the Master saw his disciple, unhappy, worried and looking extremely miserable. Recognizing his Teacher, the man burst into tears.

"Please calm yourself and tell me whatever happened to you?' said his Teacher.

"Well, Master, I did try to follow your teachings but what could I do when Maya (illusion) had me so firmly in her grasp? I now have a wife and twelve children and providing for them all is a real struggle. The responsibility for my family is becoming overwhelming.

The Master asked: "Do you realize what you have done? Not only did you make yourself miserable but also the future of your children is in jeopardy - quite apart from the fact that you seem to have forgotten everything I taught you?"

At this the disciple became rather defensive: "But Master, what could I do? This is not my fault. Maya caught me so firmly, it was impossible to get out of Maya's net. Now I need money to look after my very large family and I simply do not know how to provide."

This was a painful moment for the Master, after all this had been a promising disciple and now he was giving arguments to his Teacher. The Master decided to stay for a few days to try and help, but when it came time to leave, His disciple still did not understand. As a last lesson the Master wanted to demonstrate a point and make His disciple realize that he alone was responsible for his predicament.

The Master went to an old tree and hugging the tree firmly he sobbed and cried. The disciple heard the lamenting and approached his Teacher: "Whatever is the matter Master?" and the Teacher replied: "My son, I am helpless; this tree has caught me so completely and will not let me go."

"What — I don't understand you Master, You are such a Wise Man; how can You blame the tree? You are the one who is holding on to the tree, just let go and You will be free."

The Master looked at His disciple and said: "That is exactly what I want to tell you. You alone are responsible for your situation and only you can free yourself — after you have taken care of your family now."

It should be understood that in life the Sat Guru will give you the key to open the right door along the path. It is imperative that you take responsibility for your progress, whether He is physically with you or not in times of decision making on life's journey.

The Sat Guru relationship is a concept which can also become confused. In various countries in the western world, courses are being advertised that after six weeks training you can obtain a "guru certificate". A rather different course takes place in India, when after twelve years of learning, the Sat Guru says "not yet ready", you will face another twelve years of tapasya, of practice and penance. The kind of western qualification is out of the question. In some countries "anything goes" and the impact is felt throughout the world. The popular magazine TIME produced a positive article about yoga a few years ago. Surprisingly, only after this article appeared many people in India started doing yoga, although yoga and meditation have existed for thousands of years and had always been an integral part of Vedic life. Only after the article it became something like fashion. Today you will find yogic instructions on every TV channel in India. Yet all this only took place after the approval by Time Magazine. People were not aware but rather caught in a kind of slavery of mind. "Slave" mentality is an insidious aspect of a mind enslaved by stereotypes and limitations. It takes a long time to escape from mental slavery, where you have no creativity or innovation. You may serve while the Master is present, but as soon as the Master is gone, you fall back into the old habits. The saying "When the cat is away, the mice will play" sums it up nicely.

While caught in slave mentality it takes a long time to reach emancipation and freedom. People have programmed themselves to have no mind of their own. If you do not have the mind to create and think for yourself you are a slave. You can also be slave to your own desires, to the lowest level of your mind and body. Slavery comes in many different forms. Yet you want freedom and emancipation from your own bondage, to be a prisoner no longer.

This is where the Sat Guru can break down your cycle of conditioning and negative programming. This can lead to intense re-examination and change which is vital in the Dark Age that most of this world is caught up in. If you are on the path and seeking enlightenment you must listen to the Sat

Guru. The concept of the Sat Guru is such that you grow, learn and experience your divine being, you experience a different pulse, the energy of spiritual vibration when you are tuned to that higher energy.

To illustrate the need for surrender to such higher energy, personified by the Sat Guru it is helpful to recount the story of the great Tibetan Yogi Milarepa:

A long time ago, in the 11th century there lived a young man in Tibet by the name of JetSun Thopaga. His parents were prosperous and he and his younger sister Peta could look forward to a promising future. However, nothing can be taken for granted and by the time Thopaga was 7 years old his father fell ill and died. His aunt and uncle, previously the poor relations, became the guardians of the children and administrators of the estate.

Let it be said that this turn of events resulted in abject misery and ill treatment for the widow and her children. Not only were their lands usurped, but the fatherless family was reduced to going hungry and wearing rags for many years.

Thopaga grew and by the time he had grown to be a youth he had had enough of the manipulations and lies of his aunt and uncle. With his mother's encouragement he decided that something had to be done to avenge his father's legacy and the thought of becoming a black magician occurred to him as a most appealing solution. In due course he found a suitable master of the dark arts and Thopaga became his most adept student, wreaking havoc on his enemies by his 'specialty' of creating fierce hailstorms which brought total destruction to the fields of his relatives. This worked all very nicely for some time. However, Thopaga could not tune out his conscience; he was keenly aware of the law of compensation, the law of karma. He knew that one day he would have to pay dearly for the misery he had caused.

After agonizing contemplation, he knew that in order to be relieved of this debt, he would have to find a Master who could free him from guilt and deliver him from the karmic repercussions of his ill deeds.

He had heard of Marpa, the Translator and of this Teacher's reputation of being an enlightened Lama. So he set off to find Lama Marpa and to ask for the teachings of how to make up for his life of causing death and destruction, offering willingness and resolve to devote himself to a life of Truth.

Marpa and his wife Demema took JetSun Thopaga in and Marpa promised to teach him - eventually. However, the Lama proved to be a very hard task master and started the former sorcerer of by making him build a house. When almost finished, Marpa inspected the site and told His disciple: "No good, oh Master of the Black Arts, knock it down again and take the stones to where you found them."

JetSun was troubled, but he had to do as the Master instructed. Barely finished with this task, Marpa proclaimed: "I still need this house; now go and build me a decent house." Again, shaking his head in resignation, our former sorcerer set to work and started building another house.

Yes, and again Marpa checked the progress of this house: "Can't you do anything right? This is all wrong, tear it down and take the stones to where you found them!"

"Master, my hands a bleeding and I have sores on my back from carrying the stones, I cannot go on"

"Well, you have no choice, if you want My teachings you had better get on with it. You can see My wife and she will give you a salve to put on your back - and then when you are done, you must build Me a house that is fit for Me and My family, not the huts you were creating so far."

Thopaga had had enough. "This is not a teacher, he thought, "this is a cruel sadist, he takes delight in creating misery, he promises to teach me and never does. I will have none of this any longer". He poured out his troubles to Demema, Marpa's wife, who promised to help him. So he left, with a forged letter of introduction to another Teacher, a former disciple of Marpa's who instructed JetSun in meditation. It was only when it became apparent that the new disciple was not making any progress, that Thopaga confessed the forgery of the letter. His new Teacher made it clear to him that he had to go back to Marpa and impressed upon the renegade pupil that there was none more qualified as a Teacher than Marpa the Translator.

JetSun did return and finally he received initiation from Marpa. Thereafter, having completed many years of hardship and austerities the former Black Arts Wizard, now called Milarepa, (the one who wears white cotton) attained the state of complete enlightenment. The cave where Milarepa meditated, living on nothing but nettle tea, which gave his skin a green color (as seen is some paintings); have been preserved to this day.

The lesson that speaks from this example is that a human being has no idea — cannot begin to fathom — the mystery of God's working. Only a true Master can evaluate the conditioning of a person's mind and what it takes to overcome, to break it.

* Narayan was the first Sat Guru, Sat Guru also refers to Supreme Being.

Chapter

11 Managing the World Crisis

When you practise meditation, pranayama and other spiritual practices you benefit physically, mentally, psychologically, psychically and of course spiritually. Such benefit can be felt on many levels. Patanjali, the great compiler of the Yoga Sutras and the Eightfold Path of Yoga arranged, and integrated these techniques in such a way that there is comprehensive benefit for the human being. When you do pranayama, for instance, it regulates the energies within your body; it returns the heart to a normal rate, it regulates your blood pressure and much more.

Chanting also has a similar effect on the mind; chanting done every morning and before going to sleep will benefit you on all levels. If you practice such techniques regularly you will be able to perceive the wide-ranging effect throughout your system. Chanting is a very powerful technique, invoking the energy trapped within you — the perennial sound. Kabir, the great mystic and High Being was very blunt at times and did not hesitate to tell the Truth, preferring to tell it as it is, rather than going around in circles. He hit hard where it hurt most to break the resistance of the ego, tearing down the veil of ignorance. He said: "Oh deaf one, can you not hear the eternal sound; oh blind one can you not see the eternal light, and oh fool, why can you not meet your Beloved who is sitting right there within you?

Kabir thus challenges people by calling them deaf, blind and foolish, because they cannot see, they cannot hear and they do not realize that who and what they are searching for is right there within. That is the tragedy of the human being. Krishna says: "Remove your veil and meet your Beloved." The perennial or eternal mystic sound within you is the ultimate king of all sounds; the most beautiful music of the world is just nothing in comparison. By evolving yogis hear that eternal and intoxicating sound.

All the truly talented and inspired musicians have been given part of a secret gift, although none have been given the whole secret. Imagine yourself in a concert hall with the most beautiful acoustics all around you, then multiply the beauty of such sound many, many times to glean some idea of the divine sound within and around you.

European civilization developed primarily to satisfy the physical senses. All the great masters of Europe were considered no more than entertainers somehow; entertainers for the general public and especially for royalty. Thus they were rewarded for the entertainment value they provided. Because of such materialistic 'demotion' many great artists and masters were most unhappy about the lack of true appreciation of their music.

In India however, music has always been a spiritual practice and medium for self-realization. Generally music in India is often connected with a deity. Sarasvati, goddess of knowledge, music and the arts is depicted with her Vina as is Siva with his famous drum the Damaru. Siva is considered the originator of great music. All art forms in India such as music, poetry, crafts, evolved through spiritual understanding. Artists thought that their particular achievement would lead to enlightenment. Yet did any of the famous western musicians even consider enlightenment? That is the real cultural tragedy, that this beautiful gift of nature, this gift of God which has been given to you, has not been utilized to achieve its true meaning.

Imagine that some High Being is on a mountain and gives you the ladder that you may climb to come and join Him. But you ignore the ladder and do not use it to uplift yourself. That is how I feel about modern society. So many gifts have been given, yet people do not realize that such gifts are clues, secret signs or keys that help you to resolve problems and uplift yourself. These are generally regarded as inventions and useful discoveries. That is why one has to appreciate how things developed in traditional India.

There is a small story to illustrate the kind of powerful energy that can see God in any creature. That kind of intensity is missing in today's world.

There once was a High Being, who lived in the forest, tending a little shrine. Every day it was His custom to cook delicious food, which He ritually offered to God in the little shrine where God was supposed to dwell. Allowing some time for God to have "finished the meal", the food is distributed between the devotees as prasad, blessed food.

One day the Master was intent on arranging the food with the utmost care, having prepared the vegetables and the roti. It is custom to add a little clarified butter, ghee to the roti for taste as well as to make the bread nice and soft and to add a touch of "purity". Everything was ready but as the Master went to get the ghee, a large dog came by, and, snatching the entire stack of bread, ran off with it.

Well, the Master, in hot pursuit, ran after the dog, calling out: "My Lord, please wait, please wait and let me put the ghee on the roti" and thus continued running after the dog. It was a long chase until, at the point of complete exhaustion, the Master finally collapsed. And legend relates that God appeared to Him in the form of the dog, telling Him: "I am pleased with your dedication and devotion — no one has ever done that."

It is at the height of devotion, that you may be able to truly "see". No matter what culture you live in, or what your concept of God may be, humans create a concept of some power greater than themselves. If you have to create a concept of that power, which you might call God, why not create a concept which is beautiful and fulfilling, a concept whereby you can uplift yourself? The gift to uplift yourself by many different means is given unconditionally; there is no condition attached what.ever. Yet time and again you fail to appreciate the gift and do not utilize that gift to help yourself to evolve.

Nowadays much political talk is about global warming and global poverty. The vast majority of the world population is poor and starving. Yet all the suffering, pain and torture people inflict on each other in ignorance is created by them unnecessarily. That is my point: only when ignorance is removed can enlightenment follow, and a return to the golden age. As long as ignorance prevails, however, there will be more exploitation, engendering more ego, then again more exploitation, followed by ever more suffering, and more pain. Only if ignorance is removed, will ego and exploitation also vanish; the mighty 'I am': King, Queen, Prime Minister, President, this, that and all the other labels people have attached to themselves and their environment will cease to exist.

One well known man I met explained to me that he had made a lot of money in his life and yet he felt empty and unhappy. Fortunately for him he was able to realize that his was a spiritual emptiness and this realization offered him a chance to change. He was aware that he could only feel rich when spiritually fulfilled. But how many truly wealthy people realize that their unhappiness is related to their spiritual poverty?

When we make the statement: "I am this, I am that" then a mountainous ego makes its appearance followed by a huge facade and this creates ever increasing gaps between people. However, if following Vedantic teachings, people can instead say "I am Brahman (Aham Brahasmi) the Ultimate, and Absolute — and so are you, (Tat Tvam Asi)" Such statements can only be made on the purest level. When, on the material level — on the basic human level — you say: "I am this or that", then you create an ego like a balloon, which, filled with air, only needs one pin prick to deflate it. The world has a puffed up ego and when you do not realize who you actually are, then that ignorance leads to a totally distorted perception of what is and who you are.

Your perception is important, how you perceive and how you discriminate. Once your perception is right, there will be no problem. It is like mathematical calculations; you cannot be half right and half wrong. So once you get your numbers right, all is right and all is well.

The world is going through many crises. People need to learn to talk to each other, to communicate within cultures and belief systems. The world is a global village today: events in any part of the world are noted everywhere else. You are exposed to the world and there is no escape. You cannot hide, you cannot escape and you are cornered. You need to have debates and face the Truth although many people in the world are governed by their fears. You may have held a belief for most of your life and suddenly it is proved wrong, highlighting your ignorance. Since it is the nature of things to change and to be in transition and evolution you have to examine and re-evaluate everything continuously.

In a recent article in Time Magazine someone raised the question: 'Do we need religion?' Until recently no one really wanted to deal with this topic. It seems that there is some interest now to examine our believe system. We need many new definitions and clarification including the concept of God.

The world is at a critical stage and so far people have avoided key topics. In future there will be no other choice but to discuss human understanding of all kind of issues. During an open debate a lot of things will emerge. Vedanta encourages you to question: Why are you here, what is your purpose, why are you doing anything? Use your physical faculties to examine these questions. Contemplate: what are we all doing to each other today, what do we want and why?

To reach a solution there has to be a universal debate; everyone needs to participate, not just a select few. In the meantime you should find your own solution. Look at whatever problem you may have before anyone else has to tell you. It is better to be your own teacher rather than someone else having to tell you what to do. Become your own true teacher where you can apply the knowledge. Secrets and formulae have been given to help you become self-sufficient. Such 'secrets' are actually fundamental human rights; they are not trade secrets which are closely guarded to prevent financial loss. In spirituality however, there are no financial concerns, there is no money. The only currency is caring love.

Chapter 12

Breaking Free of Your Programming

Consider this: You are the creator of your body and your mind, of your senses, knowledge and wisdom; you have created everything that you have and that you are: you are your own creator.

In this approach, then what is the role of God? According to many beliefs the definition of God is that He/She is omnipresent, omniscient and omnipotent. Do you have those qualities or are they only reserved for God? Can you imagine experiencing such qualities? For instance, you may visualize meeting Siva, Buddha or Jesus. If they were to manifest, how would you behave or interact?

You may have been raised with the concept of how a guest is supposed to be greeted: you are programmed to offer something. You may perceive yourself as very sophisticated or civilized. You may think that, but in fact you have been programmed from the time of your birth.

You have been told that you are this, that and the other, to do one thing, and not the other. All this is programming from your parents, your family, your schools, friends and your environment. For some time you behave accordingly, and then one day the time comes that you want to break free.

Take the example of hypnotism or mesmerism: It is said that the subject has to consent to be hypnotized or mesmerized effectively. Both methods have become established therapies for treating physical and emotional problems. The problem is that such methods can be misused. When you have consented to be controlled and manipulated, to be used and sometimes abused, to think in a particular way or to believe and accept certain concepts, you have handed over your own power of discrimination.

This is often also the case in relationships, when you empower someone else. You may empower each other to the extent that there is a battle of wills. Both parties battle to take control, and which partner finally wins remains to be seen. This continues and it can become a battle for life. It is an insidious and enervating game which is played constantly: everyone participates in this great game of maya - illusion. A vivid example is in the context of families where children move on from any disagreement while adults dwell and create more suffering.

Thus people play games in an unending pattern. Perhaps this is how it should be as part of lila, the Cosmic or Divine Play. Vedanta states that nothing is to be rejected; that everything is recycling, constantly changing, forming and reforming; merging, integrating, and disintegrating.

You have been given a gift of planet Earth and the Cosmos. What do you do with it? You can make it beautiful or ugly. You may have the most stunningly beautiful landscapes of forests, lakes, deserts and mountains, yet somehow manage to spoil all this beauty with the ugliness of billboards and other squalid examples that blot the lovely landscape.

Moreover what do you do with your body? The physical body represents your personal planet. How do you manage it, how do you take care of it? When you learn to utilize your body for your own growth then you can make positive changes. It is important to consider human conduct or behavior. Would it not be nice to have people come to your door asking: what can I do for you today? Would it not be fulfilling to offer help when need is noticed, or to receive comfort when you are down? It takes so little effort; why are you reluctant, why consider it a burden to be nice to each other? What is it that makes you so miserable? You need to look at this, recognize it as unhealthy behavior and weed it out before it does more damage. You are allowing the weeds of negativity to grow within you, you are allowing them to gain a stranglehold on you, thereby killing all the beautiful flowers and taking over your garden. The result is that you are sad, depressed, and full of sorrow and pain.

You have been given a choice; it is your freedom, it is up to you how you wish to create your garden. This is your problem, not God's nor anyone else's — it is your problem on how you chose to live and how you can bring yourself to your destiny. You may pollute your body and mind and your planet, but nature has a different way of coping. You would not want nature to deal with your problem. Yet when you really cannot handle your problem, nature will do so, and nature's way will be extreme. It will be such an extreme that you would never want nature to intervene in your problem.

Look at the example of how nature deals with a problem: Let us say that you have a six-foot body that has been polluted, used and abused, a body full of disease, pain and suffering and all the negativities you can think of: you have so used and abused the body that it has come to the brink of non-existence. Then what will happen eventually? It dies - prematurely. Finally, when put into the extreme heat of cremation what remains? A tiny pile of ashes — and six feet of human body have been reduced to six inches of dust. Such is nature's way of taking care; there is no pollution in sterile dust and finally, by throwing it into the wind, all is gone.

The higher the heat, the less quantity of substance. If nature has to deal with this planet, it can be reduced into a few handfuls of ashes. This is the reality: nature has the power. It is a shocking reality and we do not want to think of such unpleasantness, as seen in the debate over climate change and the documentary 'An Inconvenient Truth', an appropriate term. No one wants the truth, it is inconvenient and troublesome and people avoid it. For instance any talk about the changing environment will affect the economy and is therefore unpopular. It is often the same with religion and God. There are subjects which people prefer to avoid, such as death. It is the human tendency not to discuss anything perceived as unpleasant.

As I said before, people empower others to take care of their problems. That is the way the world is governed: by empowering each other. How to empower the right person? Take charge and become wise. Know what you are dealing with. Do your homework. Arm yourself with knowledge, then you can face any situation. Knowledge will make you free - truth too, but truth can also get you into trouble in the world of maya.

The sad thing is that at times you have to manipulate and hide your own truth - especially when it becomes "inconvenient". It is a tragedy that you have to hide the truth many times, that you cannot share many things; that if you speak your mind and heart you will be ridiculed. You will be laughed at and mocked because others do not understand. Or you will be censored and punished.

People like to place you in a proverbial 'box' and once you are put in a box it is difficult for you to get out. Society expects you to conform and if you do not, you are in trouble. Therefore, beware of what box you might 'check', watch what you sign, for if not carefully selected you can sign yourself into real trouble. This is the world of contradiction and conflict, yet collectively you have all created this world: you cannot blame anyone but yourselves.

Sometimes you may want to pretend to be what you are not because you do not recognize yourselves. People want confirmation of everything they are doing, at times in the form of clichés. You forget that you have to discard the baggage you carry. You cannot climb the mountain and reach the summit while carrying all your trappings on your back, which is like a collection of all you have gathered over lifetimes. On the path to enlightenment you want to be lighter, not heavier. Lighten your load; get rid of all your accumulated attachments.

Kabir says: "The house of your Beloved is very far and the path is very narrow". If it is so narrow how can you take all your things with you? You need to be 'slim' and fit to navigate such narrow path. Literally it is in your hands on how you discriminate between what is helpful and what is a hindrance for you.

Nature and High Beings have given you much knowledge; the problem is that there is not enough practice! Do not turn your Teacher into an entertainer and magician. Implement His teachings instead.

Chapter

13

Renewal of Happiness

Visualize yourself on a beautiful spring day when all is new and fresh, green and blossoming. The birds are singing and all is bright. Singing is a form of happiness and when you are happy, time becomes unimportant. You can be happy any time you choose. By the same token unhappiness is also in your own hand. Consider how quickly just one thought can make you really unhappy when remembering some unpleasant event, incident or personal interaction. One single thought of the past can make you so unhappy — and there is no shortage of unhappy events. Nevertheless, equally there is plenty of material in life to recollect and to make you happy. Either case is essentially a frame of mind. Eventually you are the one to decide whether to be happy or unhappy. You are the sum of all your past impressions today; you are the resulting end product. Whoever they are, everyone is a product of his/her past. It is like swimming in turbulent waters you can either go along with the flow or you can struggle against the flow — downstream or upstream, the choice is yours.

Spring has so many varied and lovely aspects that it is difficult to get tired of it. While all seasons are special, spring is truly a gift of nature. You have been given so many gifts, but do you appreciate all the beauty that is given? Do you make good use of all the precious gifts? Life itself is a great gift: do you value your life? Life has been given to you for a purpose: to learn and to improve yourself and your environment. Some people feel that the world is very negative and are so focused on the prevailing negativities that they do not wish to come back to this world. Then the question arises: who created the negativity? There is collective and individual creation. You could say that there are two worlds: one consisting of chaos, conflict, ugliness and suffering. This is the material world in which all struggle. Yet there is also another world, full of beauty and joy, happiness and peace, fulfillment and love. These are the endless gifts of life and both worlds are presented to us.

In the Bhagavad Gita, when in emotional crisis and turmoil, Arjuna asked Krishna: "What is the difference between you and me?"

Krishna says: "Not much - on the physical level we are very much the same, but the real difference becomes apparent when you go deeper. Arjuna, I am seeing and yet not seeing, I am talking and yet not talking. In all my activities, whatever I do I am doing and yet not doing." Vedanta says that if you identify with your activities, making you the doer, you are in trouble. Before you say: I am doing this or that, have you tried to find out who this you is? Is it your body; is it your mind, your ego, or your intellect — who actually is this doer?

Remember this: if you identify with what you are doing, you also become responsible for the results. But when you have the capacity to observe and comprehend, to really understand, then whatever is presented to you is a gift of life. When you live in the world of positivity — when duality does not affect your mind and you can keep your balance and remain in control of yourself, and when no one can disturb you — then you are able to perceive the way things are and should be. Then happiness can be yours at any time you wish. A common mistake is to think that one day you will be happy once various criteria are attained: that is not the case.

There is no 'time table' for joy and happiness, whether morning, noon or night. When you program yourself to work on yourself so that you are able to inspire yourself and others, things will become much easier. Sometimes I feel I need to inspire people regularly, like a big clock that needs rewinding every week, although some need it daily or - when defective - every hour.

It would be nice to inspire people more long-term. Everyone has inbuilt energy, but you forget who you are and what you can do. How can you rejuvenate yourself? There are so many beautiful signs are all around you. Like springtime, nature gives you the opportunity to meditate on the beauties of the season and its joy. It is truly a symbol of happiness and rejoicing. Try to look forward to spring and happiness, not just once a year but any time. The beauty of nature is that you do not have to wait for happiness. Look at the many different reasons you have to be happy, both externally and internally. To be happy at all times is a technique that has to be learned. The process of meditation is to attune to your true Self. Like an engine that is out of tune people can have erratic and unpredictable behaviors. Tune your personal engine to your own true Self. When your mind, intellect, senses and emotions are working in harmony all your relationships become balanced. There will no longer be any conflict, duality or negativity. All you will experience is balance, and that will be part of your future, the sum of your achievements.

From the time you are born until the age of sixteen is the time in which the sum total of your personality is formed.Of course changes can take place at any time. That is the freedom you have, to reprogram yourself at any time. But you have to be a Master to be able to change your program, like a Jnani, a wise person. That 'personality' becomes part of your genetic information, and that genetic code in turn will also be transferred to a child you may have. When we get exposed to new ideas, both negative and positive, the brain records everything and the information becomes part of the brain's commandment. For instance, when engaged in pranayama, the message is sent to the brain. From there the information is relayed to the various organs, where changes can be made. It is a very complex system. That is why knowledge and wisdom become such very important factors.

The world of maya (illusion) will never be perfect; it is a composition of perfections and imperfections. There are constant fluctuations of negativity and positivity. If you think that one day the world will be perfect and therefore you will be perfect, forget that thought; it will never happen. That is a law of creation. Some phases of time are more pleasant and positive whereas others are not as good, depending on the Vedic tradition of a particular yuga. Yugas* manifest in cycles. There is Satya Yuga, the golden age of truth, then Treta Yuga, Dwapara Yuga, and finally Kali Yuga, the mechanical age of machinery, full of negativity and conflict. After completing the cycle of all four ages, this is supposed to be followed by your liberation and total emancipation which is within the soul.

Within that concept, thinking in terms of total freedom, the conditioning of time no longer exists. The concept of time is limited in the physical sense; there is no concept of time in the spiritual realm. It is like living in two parallel worlds, one external and one internal, yet living in both worlds at the same time and knowing each one.

Let us come back to the example of springtime; it is so pleasant that you look forward to its beauty. Similarly you also do not get tired of spirituality. Like an inner spring of life spirituality promotes a spring-like feeling of coming alive. It is important to nurture this feeling, and although each season has its beauties, especially if you are attuned, you will enjoy everything and there is nothing to be rejected. It is all a recycling process. What you reject returns to you in different form, nothing is wasted.

Each thought is recorded in the Akashik Records. One day the technique to unfold knowledge may be so advanced that computers are no longer necessary. All you have to do is meditate and tune into whatever record is desired. One day you may open your laptop, but in the meantime, Google is not yet connected to the Akashik Records! Those questions are not yet answered by any search engine.

In the meantime remember that you are all students of life on this earth, constantly learning and updating your knowledge and having to "take your exams" and face the challenges. Just consider when the day comes that you face your Creator or true Self how will you account for yourself?

The real qualification is the Supreme Knowledge - once you have that, all becomes crystal clear. There will be no more questions, no more confusion, doubt or misery. Once you get to this place, there will be no return and no regret.

* See chapter 10

Chapter

14

Recycling Your Life

Sometimes people express confusion about how to chant a mantra, devotional song or a prayer. Actually there are three correct stages of chanting:

1. Chanting out loud;
2. Just moving lips and tongue;
3. Only with your breath.

Although all methods are effective, focusing on your breath while repeating a mantra is especially helpful when the mind is disturbed. Loud chanting can actually help calm a disturbed mind. The repetitive sound will create vibrations within the mind and activate the energy in Sahasrara Chakra on the top of the head thereby triggering different energies in the body.

In India there is endless freedom to practice religious and spiritual rituals according to your understanding and choice — some may worship Siva, Krishna, Brahma, Durga, Hanuman — it is a very wide selection of choices.

There are also people who do not worship in form but choose the formless God - no one is bound to follow a particular discipline. Worship is conducted according to your own temperament and your own ability to relate to the subject of your devotion. There is great freedom as well as great responsibility. You try to use those energies to enhance your own growth and level of understanding.

Example: You are someone who is a devotee of Krishna and you want to attain Krishna Consciousness. How do you achieve this? How do you elevate yourself to that level? Do you want to bring Krishna down to your level or do you want to uplift yourself? Various methods and approaches are available - one of the effective ways is to have a Mansic Puja, a mental worship where your entire consciousness is focused on the image of the deity or the Master, thereby creating a connection to that Being.

To clarify this principle on the very mundane level: if someone likes tea for instance, you may invite that person for tea. Again you have created a connection. If you want to invite someone, you focus on that person's interests.

Krishna devotees may sit in meditation, drawing an image in their minds whereby they visualize Krishna sitting in front of them. A further stage in the mansic puja is:

- visualizing washing the feet of Krishna with water;
- taking flowers and fruit as offering;
- applying chandan to the feet and;
- completing the puja with Arati.

Thereafter people may ask for blessings, surrendering body and mind to Krishna.

Asking for His presence in your life through the practice of Mansic Puja — inner meditation — is relatively easy because you are doing something; you are engaging in a particular act. If you are not doing anything, that makes it much more difficult; you need to engage your mind in some form of interaction. Having established that, meditation becomes easy.

If you are fortunate enough to come into contact with a living Master or Teacher, this is the easiest and most effective meditation. You do not have to create the scene; He/She is already there. All you have to do is to replay in your mind that which has already been experienced. It is the easiest form of meditative practice — it is very effective and it can be done at any time.

When you replay all that, what happens then? Is it just a fantasy of mind? Let me explain this principle once again. Let us say that you recall some incident in your life and some unpleasant thought is recalled. Instantly you become very angry. Then you recall and replay the situation in your mind. May be you think that you should have acted or replied differently, or you may feel that you have been mistreated, unjustly criticized or insulted by somebody. Whichever way, instantly there is a very strong emotional and even physical reaction: your blood pressure shoots up, you become tense, your heart is racing, your breath is fast and irregular — your entire body is affected.

By the same principle, when you replay the nice and beautiful aspects of your life's experiences, this is bound to create a positive outcome of thoughts, feelings and vibrations, making you feel wonderful.

Many people ask how they can be happy. Actually, it is very easy to be happy; everybody has had happy events and moments in life. It is up to you to recall and replay those instances. You can re-visit those occasions and when you do, you will see the results. Even while you focus on the happy, nice and positive aspects, the negative moments may also be lurking nearby. They are part of your life too. In that case you need to learn how to avoid those pitfalls and remain focused on your happy path.

The point is that your life has a lot of answers. It can serve as your teacher, but you have to find the teachings. It is a bit like going into the forest and learning to pick the right mushrooms, avoiding the inedible and poisonous ones. Not everything that is 'green' is safe. This is something you have to learn.

There is also a way of looking back to moments in your life in order to understand how you can recycle your unhappy experiences. What was bad and what was good? Something appearing as negative can actually be quite helpful. How can you 'recycle' your mind so that you can benefit from all experiences? Each incident you are presented with is an opportunity to examine yourself, the situation in question and the other person involved. Why did this happen to you, how can this benefit you or enrich your life? Getting stuck in one particular incident can prevent you from being able to move further.

All the rich experiences of your past should make you wiser; learn to let go of dislikes and emotions and of negative thought patterns. Instead, learn to look at the benefits of your experiences. Learn to be your life's accountant. Set up a balance sheet for your life; analyze the costs and benefits of all experiences.

Take the example of a businessman in charge of a factory. He would make a list of all the costs involved in running his company as well as a list of benefits he might reap. If the costs should outweigh the benefits, it is reasonable to assume that he would think carefully, considering whether or not to close the business.

However, an exception to justify running at a loss could be if your efforts were to serve a higher purpose. Nowadays it is quite difficult to maintain traditions based on humanitarian and spiritual grounds. Yet sometimes you just have to do that for the greater good. In such circumstances cost and benefit factors do not really apply.

Another aspect to consider is the balance sheet of your spiritual aspirations. What benefits do you receive through your association with a spiritual Master or Teacher and what does it cost you — seva, giving up bad habits of body and mind, controlling and balancing emotions and surrendering your ego? Try to work on that balance sheet.

Essentially it is all a question of using your own resources which you do have within yourself, but you are not aware of your own inner bounty. You need to become aware of this gift. If you do not make an effort to discover the real prize you actually have right there within you, how can you realize what you have? You have what you need most readily available but you are denying the very gift you already have.

By tuning in through spiritual practices you can understand yourself and benefit in this recycling process.

Chapter

15 The Forgotten Culture

Nine types of bhakti have been described in the Vedas: among those are: Kirtanam — focusing your mind on the Supreme Being and Asmaranam-remembering. The latter refers to the memory of what has been lost and forgotten. Much has been forgotten; additionally there is a tendency to remember very selectively. You remember what is agreeable to you, what gives you comfort and what is easy. You go with the flow of whatever the prevailing tendency may be. Everyone eats, sleeps, walks, talks and deals with daily life according to the customary culture of the individual's upbringing. There are many different cultures in the world, different countries, with different habits, practices and behaviors.

There is so much more to life than your prevailing culture. You have become conditioned to the established culture of your surroundings and sadly you have forgotten your spiritual culture which is the very nature of yourself. Your physical body does not belong to any culture or country. Your body belongs to the five elements of nature which have made this body.

Your true nature is different to your learned perception. Normally you relate to your external, outside mind, which exposes you to the exterior world of your surroundings most of the time. Your inner involvement, the link which helps you to go deeper into your own being, into your source and into your true Self, that link is missing.

Researchers have recently discovered that those who meditate and have a spiritual fulfillment lead a happier life, a life which is balanced and healthy. In all positive respects such people, being attuned on a spiritual level, generally appear to lead their lives in a more wholesome way than those who live in and relate to the external world alone.

There are also those who have engaged in spiritual practice for many years, yet their conduct does not reflect this. Then the question of sincerity arises. Are you a true meditator and seeker or do you pretend to meditate and follow spiritual discipline? If you are truly sincere on your path, you will naturally benefit from your efforts. True spirituality cannot exist without sincerity. Living in the illusion of being "spiritual" can continue for many years and even lifetimes. It is like the example of a blind man who is lost in a large building and the building has only one exit. Each time he comes to the exit, he forgets to touch it and therefore misses the exit.

This is a very clear and simple example. You can miss the exit. It is the difference between one who is truly on the path and one who claims to be. The first question is: How sincere am I? Dedication is a later step. One must distinguish courses and information from sincere spiritual practices and experience. Great Yogis and Masters have achieved great heights only after much effort, discipline and hardship. Yet others claim to have instant enlightenment. If this were the case, it would make a mockery of the Yogis' sadhana and tapasya in the true perennial tradition.

Consider a seed that has been sown. That seed has to be destroyed in the process of growing further. Merging into the soil it releases its own existence, until it has become one with the elements. Then there is an 'explosion,' a transformation and what once was a little seed, now grows every day, becomes a plant and eventually a big tree, creating millions of seeds again. These seeds contain all the information, all the life energy and life force.

The little seed is like your ego; it has to merge into the whole, transform and disappear completely. Thoughts of: 'I am this and I am that' have to be left behind. This powerful little ego-seed never identifies with your true Self as long as you identify yourself as Jivatman you cannot achieve Paramatman. Ask yourself: Who am I? What am I? Why am I here? Where do I come from and where am I going? There are so many questions which you have to ask of yourself and so many questions you have to answer. Are you fulfilling this prerequisite in order to become the Paramatman. Of course the key to open the door to life's mystery is being provided, to remind you of who you are. The entire process resembles a metamorphosis of your mind and your being: a renewal of yourself. A yogi may retreat to the Himalayas for several months — or years — and emerge young and beautiful, totally renewed. You need a spiritual renewal of your own being, a transformation of soul which is an ongoing process. Your task is to take advantage of the gift you have been given and to make the best use of it. This is the forgotten spiritual culture to revive and reconnect with.

It is appropriate to have a celebration of knowledge, of life and of energy. Things will appear and disappear; life happens by its own momentum. There are so many mysteries in life. Life is an exciting journey filled with joy and happiness; it is never boring. Darkness is only the absence of light. Do not allow darkness and unhappiness in your life. Circumstances come and go; this is the way of life. The important part is not to get caught or to become victim of any situation which may present itself. You are in control and in command of your situation. You have the capability to give direction to your life and to your being. A Mystic of Punjab, Bhulleshah , once stated: "I did not know that I was the veil, that I created my own separateness. "

You alone create images and stories in your mind that can make you very unhappy. When you realize that this is the reflection of your own shortcomings you are angry at your own foolishness. Do not create phobias that have nothing to do with reality; they only make you suffer. It is the nature of mind to create continually. The mind resembles a monkey that cannot stay in one place but needs to move constantly. But you are not that monkey-mind, nor are you desire; these are your forces, your army, and you are their commander to steer the boat of your life. Once you grasp that concept, then everything becomes beautiful. This is the fascinating and interesting journey of life. The mind is made up of three elements: sattva, rajas, tamas. It is the body politics that has elected the mind to be leader. Since it is the nature of the mind to do - why not do something positive?

Now is the time to release all your negativities and free yourself from the hold of your senses, all the insecurities and fears which have held you prisoner for so long. Free yourself from the bondage of your own creations and rejuvenate your mind that you may enjoy the total freedom of your soul as you are boundless.

In essence knowledge is the most powerful tool which can make you free; like fire it will burn away all your obstacles.

Chapter 16

Finding Your Medium of Expression

A beautiful bhajan says: "My Guru is lighting the candle in me and He is removing the darkness from my heart. He is installing the light within me that brightens my heart and my soul."

When you can bring structure and harmony to your mind, thought and emotion this candle will be lit and wonderful work will result. As long as you are scattered, disorganized and in confusion, there will be problems. It is all a matter of attunement; when you are able to connect yourself to the vibrations of your Guru, the candle within you is lit and darkness is dispelled from your heart. Everything will flow and you will be able to express this light. It is an automatic process.

It is unfortunate that people have been programmed to suppress themselves. From childhood humans are taught to suppress: suppress that thought, that feeling, that very precious talent, all your emotions. Sometimes even, there is pressure to suppress your entire being with all its aspirations. In the meantime your inner soul is crying, trying to express itself. It has a desperate need to express itself. You have to find your suitable medium and the tools to express and manifest yourself which can help you to be uplifted. There are countless media of joyful expression. Children, for instance, may paint, thereby expressing the way they see the world often very differently from adults.

Music is another perfect medium for you to express yourself. It is one of the greatest and most powerful tools for humans to uplift themselves. Many spiritual masters have taken the path of music, coupled with poetry, song and dance. The famous dance, the Tandava, is Lord Siva's dance of creation. The image of Siva dancing with the Damaru, the little drum, has become well known. It is said that thereby He created the first fourteen sounds which became the basis of the first language of the universe: Sanskrit known originally as Brahmi. All other languages developed much later.

Sound becomes part of the Whole and you can express yourself through sound, through music. Through music you can become inspired. It is like opening up just as the lotus opens with the first Sun rays. Music enables you to join in the collective chorus of the universe which creates a magical effect on the mind. Music is a wonderful way to reach enlightenment by uplifting your emotions. Your very soul is uplifted through the rhythm of the sound.

Whichever means you choose, expressing yourself is very important. Whenever you are forced to suppress yourself, it creates a blockage within you which brings unhappiness. Yet when you are able to express your thought, emotion or talent, it will result in a feeling of amazing lightness. You feel so happy that everything is emerging and that you have no accumulated blockages. Indeed when you begin anything with spontaneous love, everything opens up.

The melody of life can cure you and help you recover in an expression of joy whereby you can experience the 'sound eternal'. That experience will bring harmony to your senses and emotions. Emotion is a most powerful force within you; it can resemble a flood of water which is so powerful it can destroy entire communities. Yet that same force of water can also give life. You can use your emotion to flourish, thereby bringing spring into your life, full of happy laughter — another sound where your inner self is speaking to you. It is wonderful to experience the 'incomprehensible', which cannot be grasped by normal faculties.

The challenge is to bring out this experience where it becomes alive and vibrant. You have a choice to drown in your own energy or to float above. This overwhelming energy, this awesome force of emotion, can lead you to fulfillment. That is where a mantra can help to invoke the energy within you, bringing out the accumulated and suppressed energy. Of course this has to be done within manageable means. Anything in excess can also be a problem. For instance, when you have unexpected success, the human ego can take over and become bigger than the actual success. This can lead to downfall: many people have ruined their lives because they could not handle their ego. Ego is not bad; it is a force, an energy, and when transformed into determination it can create success. Humility and love can assist you in this process.

Every now and then someone will announce that the world is to be destroyed. Well, maybe so, but then, in the last minute you get an 'extension'. The question arises: how many extensions have you received? Evidently you are still not learning. There is a proverb in India: Whenever a child is born, this indicates that God has not given up on humanity. You have had so many 'extensions' that there is truly a cause to celebrate !

There is no doubt that there is enough cause for the world to be destroyed when you consider what people have done to planet Earth, to the climate, to the environment, and what people do to each other. Consider it another gift that the Creator has a lot of patience, tolerance and love for His misbehaving children by giving them yet another chance. The example of being a parent illustrates that you have a great deal of tolerance when you have your own child. You may be critical of many things in others, but when it comes to your own child, your tolerance is amazing. You have the capacity to love and tolerate his or her nonsense where your own child is concerned.

The point is that you do have the capacity to have patience. Take the example of a close relationship: you may grumble and complain about all kinds of things, yet at the end of the day you know that you love that person and you can put aside the irritations and complaints. It is amazing how you can develop the tremendous ability of forbearance. You underestimate yourself in your ability to cope with anything in life. You do have that capability.

Life is supposed to be a celebration and there is no reason why you should not celebrate. Turn any crisis into an advantage. This is a skill you can learn by viewing the crisis as an opportunity. Begin by finding out exactly what you are dealing with, step by step:

- First, recognize that you have a problem, whether physical, mental or emotional and find out the root cause;
- Secondly, ask yourself why you have this problem;
- Thirdly, consider what you can do to resolve it ?; and
- Finally, ask what the treatment is and how to apply it.

If you deny the fact that there is a problem, the problem will not go away. Recognizing and accepting the difficulty at ground level is the basis of dealing with your trouble and that will eventually take you to mastering the crisis. There is no problem which has no solution. In fact, a solution is already in place before the problem becomes apparent. The trouble again is that we do not want to recognize and accept this fact.

Tulsidas says: "In this world we have everything, only the unfortunate ones do not receive". Therefore, make an effort to be fortunate and take what is yours. It does not matter how long you live. If the quality of your life is poor, what is the point? Ask yourself: "What is the quality of my life? Does life give me fulfillment ?"

Examine what you have created out of your life. You can build enough brightness in your life to remove all the darkness. You have every reason to be happy. Every day you have a choice to be happy. Learn to create your own happiness, your own heaven. It is all in your hands.

Chapter

17

Enjoying the Beauty

Some days are perfect days for meditation. For instance, you can visualize yourself out in the country, maybe by a lakeside, where you can integrate many of the lovely and natural environmental elements into your mind and senses. Observe the quality of wind and water, the wide openness of the sky, the warmth of the Sun, maybe a movement of trees and the lovely chatter and song of the birds. Then consider how much beauty has been provided for the human being - much more than could be deserved - so many gifts have been provided by Mother Nature and the Creator. Yet humans seem to remain ungrateful, unhappy, upset and depressed, often complaining and demanding. It would seem that there must be something in humans which is not quite right.

There is a story of the Creator, who had created the entire world and all the different creatures. As a form of quality control the Creator had also created the critic. As is the critic's wont, he found flaws with almost everything. Finally the Creator fashioned the human being, which He considered His masterpiece. He showed the carefully crafted human being to the critic. The critic slowly circled the human several times and - lost in thought for some time - he finally replied that this was indeed a remarkable piece of creation, however, there was no way of telling what was going on inside. "There is no window, he said, "I cannot see what is happening in the human's mind".

Well the critic did have a point. Mind is entirely too complex and unfortunately it is often insincere. People may come and promise the world, wanting to serve, to learn and improve, dedicate and devote themselves to the Sat Guru - the list goes on. Yet as soon as one tiny problem appears, all the emotion and devotion screeches to a sudden halt. The point is: what do you mean when you make such a statement? What is in your mind when you make this announcement? Is it temporary gratification, or is it some way to impress others? How much of your proclamation is the result of your own ego? Emotion is not devotion.

It sounds good to say "I love you"; it is nice to hear and to say. What is it that prompts you to make such a statement? It is said that actions speak louder than words. Why not act rather than make such sweeping announcements?

This is a very complex and psychological human aspect. It is so complex that you do not understand your own desires, your own likes and dislikes, your wants, your loves and hates, yet that subtle play continues. It is called the play of maya, of illusion. It is like child's play, which builds and destroys.

The problem is that you do not move on, but remain with the same thoughts and attitudes. When people have known each other for thirty or forty years, logically this should increase the bond. One should expect warmer and more caring feelings, a sense of fulfillment and attunement. Surprisingly, these things do not often happen. Instead there is resentment, frustration, quarrels and ever increasing arguments, often plain dismissal of each other and eventually severe conflict resulting in separation. Therefore, the concept of knowing someone a long time and having improved the relationship, does not always fit. The richness is missing. When you get older you are supposed to be wiser, having learned many important lessons through the years. It seems that what is supposed to be and what actually does take place are two different aspects of life.

All creatures are constantly evolving, physically, emotionally psychically and spiritually and are supposed to be reaching the point of fulfillment. Vedąnta states: 'knowledge is crystal clear; knowledge is your tool, your key to apply in all situations'. You can experiment with knowledge, whenever the situation arises, become your own teacher and guide. You know yourself best. For whenever another person directs, criticizes or instructs you, there is a tendency to become defensive and resentful. When you look at yourself objectively, you can see everything in its true light: you know where you are going and how far you have come.

It is really important that you should gather knowledge. Those who are wise employ knowledge, only the fool indulges in gossip, idle excitements and other vices. Instead, create and build your own spiritual energy!

Kabir says: "Why do I need things that intoxicate, I have my own intoxication within me". Develop your own genuine spiritual intoxication, which is the true ecstasy, whereby you view and connect with all creation. Yogis will tell you that there is an eternal music going on within you, why do you not listen to that; listen while the eternal nectar is flowing through you.

It is a pity that when something is given easily, the human being is inclined to take this for granted. When you have known someone for a long time, that connection should be growing and enriching, and become very fulfilling. Yet the evidence seems to support the opposite. Why does this happen? Yours should be an increasing and blossoming relationship, whether this is a mundane association or a spiritual relationship. Ask yourself: why did my relationship deteriorate? You have to ask yourself why your connection has lost its meaning and purpose over time. Why does my relationship not give me fulfillment and contentment? You have to examine yourself, and if anything is blocking your connection, this has to be removed. Once removed, things will begin to flow again. Relationships you build in this life are supposed to be your sadhana and like flowers, bloom and inspire, helping you to evolve, and eventually reach enlightenment.

Consider how lucky humanity is. Not only has the Creator provided you with all sorts of facilities, with all the beauty of the natural world but has also given you the chance of making contact with High Beings and Great Masters to guide you, to teach you and to lead you to the highest point. Such a great gift of Mother Nature's grace you can never repay. You have every reason to be grateful eternally. This gift is not something you can claim as your right; it is a privilege and it is a gift of compassion.

Only out of compassion will such a Being come to this world, yet humans are so limited that time and again they try to bring such a Being to their own level of mediocrity. At times there are destructive forces such as gossip and back biting. Throughout history no High Being has been spared. Look at the examples of Buddha, of Jesus Christ and many other High Beings: all became targets of corrupt human minds with devious intentions or cowardly acts. Yet when put to the test, the disciples and followers who knew who and what their Master represented disavowed the connection or disappeared from the scene. Jesus' desertion by His disciples in His hour of need is well known.

A Master can deal with the world and the people in it; there is no question about it. But when the time comes to stand by your Master, your Teacher or your knowledge, how many will remain steady?

The example of the Iranian Mystic who had been sentenced to death by stoning for his enlightened statements serves as another illustration of a disciple's fear and cowardice. As the stones were hitting his body, the Master just laughed. But when, within the gathered crowd, his close disciple picked up a flower and threw it at him, the Master began to cry. The flower of a close disciple was more painful than all the stones hurled by the crowd.

When one knows the truth and still does not follow it, there is a problem. I always say: Whenever you have a problem with anyone, talk directly to that person, not to someone else. If you have problem with A, then talk to A, not B or C. People have a tendency to talk to the wrong person instead of dealing with the one involved. This way any problem cannot get solved but it increases instead and at times it can cause unnecessary disaster.

Another incident relates to the travels of the Buddha with His disciple Ananda. During the time when the Buddha was still known as Prince Siddhartha, a princess of a neighboring kingdom wished to marry him. His refusal to comply with the lady's wishes resulted in the proverbial scorned woman's anger. Later, now as queen, she had not forgotten the insult of being denied and when informed that the Buddha was traveling through her domain, she let it be known that the traveling Master was to be demeaned and dishonored in any way possible. Ananda was disturbed and puzzled and suggested to his Master to avoid this place of trouble while traveling. "Fine, said the Buddha, "but what if the same thing will continue in other areas? You cannot avoid adversity; it would follow you the entire life. You have to deal with it and confront the problem. There is no way around it. Accept it, see how you feel, how your mind works, and know your strength."

Instead, be like the elephant that will walk, ignoring the barking dogs, because the elephant knows his own strength. You have to continue gracefully and happily without being affected while maintaining your equilibrium. That is the spiritual strength, a state of fearlessness. It only comes through spiritual inner strength and a knowledge which you have to discover within you. You have to dig into your own being like digging the earth to find this strength.

Beauty and ugliness live side by side; if your mind is stuck in ugliness you cannot enjoy the beauty. Mind can easily get caught by negativity, and then all beauty is lost to you. The choice is yours; it is up to you to decide what to concern yourself with. Why torture yourself with the negatives, when you can look instead at all the lovely things in life?

The increasing tourism to India makes this a case in point. Some tourists will only see the dirt, the beggars, the pollution, the poverty etc. Yet they totally miss the beauty derived from the historical spirituality: well-known places like Rishikesh, Benares and other locations which hold the 'footprints' and spiritual energy of sages, saints and Enlightened Beings will thus go completely unnoticed. The result is that those tourists will return empty handed, disappointed and impoverished. Well, this is the misfortune of their blindness.

You have to change your perception, make the change in your mind. It is not the world which is wrong, it is you. You have the problem; it is your mind which is mistaken if you see negativity wherever you go. If your mind is focused on positivity, you will see beauty and delight all around you.

Our little feathered friends can give you a good analogy: when you mix grains of many varieties, birds know exactly which ones to pick. It is for you to decide what is the right thing to do and which is the right thought to 'pick'. This is called viveka, discrimination which is beneficial to you. You have to develop that kind of mind to be able to see the beauty, the light and the happiness. You have to work on yourself. You have to correct yourself. Do not blame the world; it is not the world which is wrong. Instead, see beautiful things where ever you go. Darkness and light live side by side. The choice is yours.

Chapter

18 Questions and Answers Along the Path

Q: Svamiji, could you please speak about the biggest obstacles that can occur when on the spiritual path to God realization and how one can overcome them?

Svamiji: The most difficult obstacle is the conditioning of mind, for when your mind is conditioned to any thought, concept or belief, your thoughts are fixed and your attitude is somehow blocked. When you are not open to analyze, to contemplate, to understand, and to look into different aspects of the meaning and purpose of both minor and major issues, you are limiting the mind. Limitation of mind is a great obstacle. We know that the mind is not you, but that mind is part of your emotional manifestation and that it is the nature of mind to fluctuate constantly. Those fluctuations can be high or low, depending on the influence of the three gunas, the three fundamental tendencies: sattvaguna, rajaguna and tamaguna. These three qualities govern your body, mind and emotion.

- When you are in the state of sattvaguna you are creative, positive, inspired, balanced, and objective and that opens you for further development and understanding of yourself.
- In the state of rajaguna you are active, full of restless energy, passionate, with a drive to get things done, yet also prone to cravings, heated arguments, even bullying and greed.
- When in the state of tamaguna you are depressed, angry, upset, frustrated, unhappy

and confused and all the negativities are dominating your senses.

These three stages fluctuate within twenty-four hours and are also constantly affected by the outside influences of the society you live in as well as by your environment. People continually contribute to each other, especially through raja- and tamaguna, since these two qualities are prevalent in society, wherever you may go. These two gunas also present the biggest obstacles; they can actually become a trap whereby you become imprisoned by their two qualities.

On that basis you feed each other, your friends, families, coworkers, anyone you come into contact with, wherever your common interests may lie.

However, when in sattvaguna all is clear, it is like a vast clear blue sky, there are no clouds, it is all sunshine. Everything becomes lucid, you have no doubts; everything unfolds and becomes a revelation to you. Every conundrum unravels. You are self-inspired and you begin to understand 'what is what' and 'how things are'; in short, the world makes greater sense. All insecurities vanish.

The idea is to bring sattvaguna into your senses and into your life. The effect of the environment on your senses is around you all the time. Any time you go out you are affected by outside forces; then you come home and you reflect those influences on your family, who in turn will radiate the same vibrations and affect others. You cannot eliminate these influences; they are part of your creation, part of life. Nevertheless, there is a way out:

When you purposefully increase your sattvaguna with all your positive qualities, then the effect of the other two elements is greatly reduced. Thereafter you are governed predominantly by the laws of sattvaguna, which are so powerful that when you go out into society, the negative influences of rajaguna and tamaguna will simply roll off you like water off the lotus flower petals. The outside world does not affect you; you are not influenced and you are self-assured.

Now the question arises of how you can increase the qualities of sattvaguna. This is again related to how far you can raise yourself during meditation and contemplation, and how far you can analyze yourself. That comes with knowledge. Of course the grace and energy of the Master is always there to support you in this and to make things easier for your growth and understanding. However, when you have strong conditioning of mind, this is the biggest impediment of understanding the greater Self. That attitude can be like solid cement which solidifies to the extent that you cannot move and that will be the end of all growth; any chance of realization is gone. You can never just say "this is it" after any kind of revelation. Rather focus on the journey of continually growing further into your Self; the journey itself is beautiful and worthwhile, but as soon as you lock yourself into one concept or one attitude, your growth will cease and this can be the biggest challenge in your further development.

Q: Svamiji, could you please further elaborate on grace and its role and importance on the spiritual path?

Svamiji: It is said that when you take one step forward, Grace will move towards you by a hundred steps. It depends on how much you long for this Grace, how much you realize and understand. Compare this to the sunshine outside, and although you can see it, you still have to go outside to enjoy the benefit of the Sun by exposing yourself to the sunshine. Confining yourself indoors will not help.

The energy of Grace is an invisible esoteric force and when you are preparing yourself, that preparation becomes a spiritual act with all that is involved in growing and learning. You need to integrate all these forces within you to become more qualified to receive Grace.

I have often said that there is no point or value in meeting the highest Teacher or Master, if you have not evolved yourself to recognize Him or Her. For even if you meet the highest Master what is the value if you do not recognize? Before such a meeting can take place you have to prepare yourself, and in the process of your preparation you come closer to spiritual Grace. Even without noticing you will find one day that you are under the protective Grace of the Master who will lead you from one state of Grace to another and finally, when the time comes, then there will be total opening of energy, of shakti. Shakti path is the event of having Grace bestowed upon you. (In today's computer language it resembles the transmission of data onto your hard drive.) The Master can bestow energy and Grace which is like a transfer of instant knowledge, providing you are qualified. Grace is powerful energy, but before this can take place, a certain amount of development and evolution has to take place to prepare yourself for this powerful experience. You may be asked to do something apparently impossible, but when the energy of Grace is there, manifestation can take place. There after your entire development is expedited and you can approach your goal much faster.

Q: Is there a difference between Self and God realization?

Svamiji: Let us start with this statement: The human being does not know what God is. Many established religions claim to know and try to define God. However, all definitions are created by the human mind. How can you define something you do not know? Can an ant define a human being? Then the question arises of whether you have created God or whether God has created you? Either way is interesting.

The concept of God is in millions of books; trillions of thoughts have been created around God. In a way this is quite interesting; the whole humanity is asking this question. On one hand it can be easy when you say: God is there and He wants me to do this or that. So we want to make things easy to understand, and we say this is the Trinity of God; a concept which exists both in the Christian religion (Father, Son and Holy Spirit) as well as in the Hindu religion (Brahma, Vishnu and Mahesh). In some way it gives the human being some kind of comfort; you have arranged everything in a comprehensive order and because of that you feel secure. Disorder and confusion will bring insecurity and pain. When all is in order, it will bring comfort. And there is nothing wrong with it, all this is fine and it serves the purpose; but for the human being the physical reality is the only reality, although that is an illusion. After all, the physical body does not remain. There is a story to highlight the search for a different reality:

King Janaka, mighty ruler of ancient Mithila, had a dream. He dreamt that he was in a large forest, destitute and starving. Yet somehow he managed to find some plants and roots in the jungle and with great care was able to prepare a meager meal. But just as he was ready to satisfy his hunger with the modest food he had prepared, a large bull stormed into the clearing where King Janaka had made himself comfortable. Within seconds the bull had devoured every last bit of the food. The King cried in frustrated disappointment and at this point he woke up.

This dream puzzled him greatly and he wanted to know: What is the Truth? Who am I, am I the King in this palace, ruling a kingdom or am I this man lost and starving in the forest?

He wanted to find out. He invited all the scholarly pundits from far and wide to give him the answer to his question — offering half his kingdom for a satisfactory reply. Many came, after all there was the enticement of half a kingdom to consider, but alas, no one could find a suitable answer.

Finally one man stepped forward, deformed in eight joints and because of that was named Ashtavakra, (Eight Bends). All the other 'wise' men began to laugh and made derisive jokes at his deformities. Ashtavakra looked around the assembly and said: "I thought I was in the company of wise men, but now I realize that you are those who can only see the outside, the skin. Since you have only recognized my deformed body and not my Self, I cannot believe that I am in the company of astute scholars who cannot understand that "although the river may be crooked, the water never is".

Then he moved on to the King and said: "So you want to give me half your kingdom. How do you plan to do this - does it even belong to you? "

"But, yes, of course it belongs to me; I am the legal, bona fide King."

"So you think it belongs to you; before you, who owned the kingdom?"

"My father."

"And before that?"

"His father"

"After you?"

"My sons"

"So how come it was not yours before and will not be yours after you, yet in between you became the owner of the Kingdom? "

The King had to admit that there had been a flaw in his thinking and that he was actually only the caretaker of the kingdom and that it did not belong to him. Ashtavakra had made it clear to him that he could not give what he did not own.

The King puzzled for a moment, then said:
"Alright, I'll give you my body"

"Oh King, you are making the same mistake again, are you the owner of this body?"

"Yes, of course, I am the dweller of this body, therefore I own it, and everything is under my control."

"And where was this body of yours 100 years ago and where will it be 100 years from now?"

Again the King had to admit that the body did not really belong to him either and that it was just given to him on loan by Mother Nature for the duration of a lifetime, after which it would have to be returned to Nature.

"Alright, said the King, "I'll give you my mind"

"You think you own your mind; you cannot even control your mind. How can you give something over which you have no control? You tell your mind to do this and it does not even listen to you?"

In due course the King, quite defeated by Ashtavakra's logic and wisdom, said:

"Oh Master, I really must give some thought to what is really mine".

Eventually King Janaka realized that he was in the presence of a great Master, and asked to be accepted as Ashtavakra's disciple to be taught the mysteries of the Self.

The essence of the dialogue between King Janaka and Ashtavakra is beautifully rendered in the Ashtavakra Gita.

You are the Solitary Witness
of All That Is,
forever free.
Your only bondage is not seeing This.

Consider that concept, that thought of 'who am I' and 'what am I'! How can you talk about Self-realization, when you do not know what Self is? You do not know if it is body, mind, sense, or emotion, let alone knowing about God? Why not start with something you can relate to, like the body, then focus on the mind, explore the mind, then explore the senses.

Vedanta describes the difference between Atma and Paramatma - between the Self and the Ultimate. A great Persian Mystic stated: "One who knows God is not less than God" - he made that statement, considered highly blasphemous during that time, and was sentenced to death by stoning.

People gathered for the execution and it was their duty to comply with the dictates of stoning. One of the Master's closest disciples was also there and was loath to comply. He therefore picked up a flower and threw it at his Guru. During the stoning by the people the Master had been laughing, but when the flower hit him, he cried. The people were surprised and asked him: "All the stones did not seem to bother you, how come this flower upset you so much?"

"I can understand why the ignorant people throw stones at me but this man knows me, he is my disciple. His flower is more painful than all the stones."

And it does make sense, for if you know someone or something, in complete comprehension, you become that. The meditator is no longer meditator but becomes meditation; there is no longer any separation. Whatever you intently focus on, you become that. That is the law of meditation and the law of nature. Beware of what you are aiming for and what you concentrate on.

The Master's punishment was incurred by his statement that one who knows God is not less than God. Therefore, yes, Self and God are one. However, before you can come close to that goal, you have to deal with your body, with your mind and with your senses. The mind is supposed to be the charioteer to guide the wild horses of the senses. This is not easy. In the Yoga Sutras of Patanjali seekers are being guided to understand body, mind and senses. Eventually all rivers combine and become the ocean, and once they merge into the ocean they are no longer individual rivers. So you can say that the Self will merge into God.

Q: What can be done to reduce one's identification with the senses; how can one reduce their powerful influence?

Svamiji: By knowing that you are not mind and senses. I gave the example of awaking from sleep; you wake up and might say "I slept very well". Then ask: who slept and who witnessed that sleep? Any time you are engrossed in something, ask who is engrossed in the act, who is enjoying the act and who is the witness?

Some of the great Masters have given this analogy: The body is your palace, it has nine gates and the throne of your king is inside your heart - your heart chakra. This is the seat of your Beloved who is waiting for you to come to Him.

Q: How can one draw a balance between devotion to the Supreme, to the Ultimate and at the same time hold the awareness that one is Atma oneself?

Svamiji: There are three aspects: Karma Yoga, Bhakti Yoga and Jnana Yoga. All three are very important.

- Jnana Yoga is connected with the Supreme Self, with knowledge.
- Bhakti Yoga - is connected with your subtle body, with love and devotion. Bhakti is very essential as long as you are not "there". Bhakti is like a boat on which you can cross the mighty river of sansara. Even though you may focus on non-duality, you cannot do so without bhakti. Bhakti will take you to the other shore - without bhakti you can get lost. Even when evolved to the greatest height, some beings chose the approach of duality, wanting to remain bhakta, in love and reverence - although having merged into the Whole already. Only in duality can you love, love is merged in non-duality.
- Karma Yoga is connected with your body and senses- with action. You have to do Karma Yoga in any case, whether you like it or not. Whether you perform your actions laughingly or with resentment and tears, there is no escape as long as you have a body. You have to work, you have to sleep, you have to eat and clean; there is no way out. And when you do Karma Yoga with detachment you can do anything.

Q: Svamiji, could you tell us on how to deal with doubt, doubt in the teachings, in the Master, or in oneself?

Svamiji: You have to understand that doubt is of your own making, your own phobia, your confusion, your own darkness and insecurity. It is strictly a product of your own mind and fears. Do you know what you want? Make sure what you want from your life. Once you are sure about what you want, then you are clear and no one can fool you. When you have experienced the real thing you will recognize a fake. Doubt only enters when you do not know what you want. It is helpful to doubt your doubt.

Q: How can one use the power of contemplation to undo ego and identity with the senses? What is the best way to do contemplation?

Svamiji: Take the example of mixing different types of grain, lots of different types also containing small stones. When you put this mixture out into the open, birds will come and pick exactly those grains that they like. Different birds will pick different grains. They know! That is contemplation, an ongoing discrimination of what is good and what is harmful.

Q: Please speak to us of mantra, its power and the practice of it.

Svamiji: Mantra is a power seed of concentrated energy. The beej mantra, for instance, is a seed mantra and like a seed, it has all the information for becoming a huge tree when you plant it. A tiny seed can become a huge giant tree. That is what mantra is. A mantra is placed in you, observed by you, and it becomes part of you, especially when imparted by the Master. Then it grows and it can lead you to enlightenment or to any other manifestation. But mere repetition of a mantra will not work on its own.

The 15th Century mystic poet Kabir says: 'The rosary is in your hand, the lips are moving, the tongue is turning and you are repeating, yet the mind is all over the place. This is not meditation."

Mechanical repetition of mantra will not suffice, it has to be combined with other aspects and become part of your personality.

Q: Is the repetition of mantra different from focus and contemplation on the Sat Guru?

Svamiji: Yes it is different. If you focus on the Sat Guru, you are connecting with the Sat Guru and when you are repeating a mantra you are invoking the energy associated with this mantra. When you are attuning to the Master it is different although sometimes it can be combined to activate the force.

Q: What are the necessary qualities for the seeker to walk to the end?

Svamiji: Eagerness to know! To make every effort to receive knowledge followed by the necessary practices. A longing to get freedom or liberation is an essential quality. You need to be open to understand without blocking, without concluding, without imposing your thought, without any kind of conditioning. For if you are stuck in one particular concept or belief, you have created your own boundary, stopped your growth. You must break all barriers and boundaries. When you want to reach the infinite, you cannot set up finite blocks. Many seekers get stuck at one point or another due to having confined themselves. This is a pity. You should not be satisfied with the small fruit but aspire to the greater fruit.

Q: Have you seen that many seekers have been satisfied with the small fruit before the end and not go further?

Svamiji: Many times this happens, people will get the small fruit, and then they are satisfied and make no further effort in this life. They may think that they will continue in the next life.

Q; Does it also happen that some seekers achieve a certain level of evolution with genuine experiences of an altered state of consciousness and believe that they have reached the final stage?

Svamiji: Yes, this happens. Until you reach the highest state of enlightenment there can always be some delusion, confusion or misconception. That is when some people say that they hear angels speaking to them. It is difficult to ascertain how much the angels speak and how much is the person's own delusional feedback.

There can be many mixed impressions based on your own fantasies. However, there can also be genuine experiences. In the process it can happen that you may have many experiences - impressions of both past and future. Look at yourself objectively and ask: what motivates me, what makes me say, or think or do anything? All depends on the real motivation of anything you say, think or do. For instance, the statement of "I love you" has many different motivations: everybody has a different understanding, perception and expectation of love. What do people mean by that statement? What is the background thought for such a statement? Actually, it is by exploring, by finding out and defining what your motivation is in any given situation that you are moving into another form of contemplation.

Q: Svamiji, could you please speak to us about the subject of relationships, especially intimate relationships, while on the spiritual path? How do they affect human growth and what is the appropriateness and value while striving for enlightenment? Is there a way to avoid the pain and suffering that frequently accompanies a relationship?

Svamiji: Primarily you need a strong signal that can help you to communicate. Interaction and communication are very important. If you have a beautiful experience, it is natural that you may want to share this experience and knowledge. Many people are miserable. How is one to make them happy? I see all the suffering and pain. The whole purpose of My being in this world, of having manifested in duality, in body, is to show people how to overcome their unhappiness and suffering, to show them the path to happiness, to enlightenment.

Q: Where is it helpful for one's spiritual goal to be in a relationship and where is it a hindrance?

Svamiji: If the gap of consciousness between two people is too big then it can be a hindrance because then you are dealing with different expectations. There is no attunement and therefore communication is obstructed; it is not a parallel journey. A relationship needs to be synchronized, like the cogs in a machine to function as a unit. When you are not synchronized in your minds, expectations are not the same and the relationship becomes mutually unfulfilling and will eventually fail.

If a couple can discuss their relationship problems objectively and each is willing to listen to the other, really listen, with tolerant understanding, then there is a possibility of coming to a workable compromise. When both partners are willing to let go of the many unimportant issues that each one has built up and is so hung up on, and when each partner can look at those personal things that are not good for the partnership, and decides to let go, progress can be made. One very important aspect in resolving disagreements is self-analysis and self-correction. This is important, for you cannot overcome conflict by justifying and defending the prompts of your ego and your emotions. I recommend for everyone that, before you go to sleep, to take five or ten minutes to analyze your day, and note where you have done anything that is not helpful to you. Then make sure you do not repeat this.

The emphasis is on self-analysis; it has to be done by oneself, for if brought up by others, justification, excuses and finally anger will result. Ego is the main personality here. It is strange that people often prefer to be right than to be happy. Ego is always there, in many different guises. Someone may try to provoke you into reacting to a perceived criticism and tell you: "you should not tolerate this." You may agree and act in response, rather than thinking for yourself, exploring that other person's motivation and finding out yourself. It needs courage, coupled with being perfectly honest and true to yourself. You cannot progress spiritually if you are not honest with yourself. That is the basic requirement. Do not fool yourself, do not pretend. You may pretend your whole life that you are this or that - but it does not make it so. It is actually far too much work; pretense and ongoing lies can become a very stressful exercise. You need to have courage to be rigorously honest with yourself.

In Vedanta, the Brahma Sutra states: "The weak person cannot come to Me. Only the strong can come to Me. This refers to inner strength and courage. The knowledge that what you are doing is worthwhile, knowing that a greater reward is waiting for you and that you do not want to miss this, will achieve and build inner strength. It is a great pity if you miss this opportunity.

Q: Svamiji, could you talk to us about what happens after death?

Svamiji: This depends on what level of consciousness you were at the time of leaving the body. Many and various aspects come into this; each individual is unique with a different state of consciousness. Any attachments you have formed in your life, you will carry with you. For example, if you leave your body while still being attached to all your worldly things, something you have built over many years, this will carry over and your soul cannot be liberated. Remember, you have three different bodies: the physical body, the subtle body and the astral or causal body.

When you die, only your physical body is discarded. The subtle body does not die; it carries all your impressions and it remains - depending again on the type of person you were. The astral or causal body simply merges back into the Whole, resembling the confining walls of one smaller space dissolving into the higher and greater space, into the Whole and becoming part of That. However, although you are not the subtle body, since you have identified yourself with it - being the intellect, mind, ego and emotion - that part will continue.

So, what is the relationship between the three bodies? Take the example of the Sun. The Sun has no connection with the earth and is not affected by the earth, yet the earth depends upon the Sun. Your physical body is the earth and the Sun is the Atman, the Self, which is reflecting on the body through the subtle body. Although the Self is not connected in any way, yet the physical body very much depends on it. When that light comes, both physical body and subtle body are activated.

In the case of Enlightened Beings, it makes no difference whether they have a body or not because they have consciousness. In their physical bodies, the subtle body is transient and since they have never identified with the subtle body, both physical body and subtle body are destroyed when they leave. The physical body of an Enlightened Being is created for the purpose of communication with the human being, by descent into human form. Thus a descending being is actually divinity in form. Such a Being may look human, but is not human. One who is striving is an ascending being. Enlightened Beings may have a physical and a subtle body, which really make no difference since they have everything and do not long for anything. When you know what you can manifest, you do not have any longing. It does not matter where you are, in a cave, palace, seaside, or wherever.

Enlightened Beings may appear like human beings but their perception is totally different. There is no duality. When a spiritual being falls down, it means that he/she had not achieved that final state. But once you have gone beyond that final barrier, there is no question of falling down; there is no ego, no desire. If an Enlightened Being should display some of these tendencies, it is more like a form of play, for the sake of the human being.

You ask what is the last thing to go before liberation. It is always attachments: attachment to places, attachment to personal things and attachment to persons; these are the three things that have to be overcome. The final and most difficult thing to go is attachment to thought. This is the biggest and the most difficult thing to let go. To be able to let go of any kind of thought is the final hurdle.

Chapter 19

Life is a Journey

Life is a journey you have embarked upon. At each step there is a new revelation. You deal with both day and night, light and dark, joy and pain. When you truly recognize yourself, you cannot reject yourself - darkness also becomes light.

Children are often scared of the dark, yet when playing in the dark as a part of a game, somehow they can deal with the darkness. Darkness is only threatening as long as you are outside of darkness - once you enter darkness, it becomes familiar. It is the same with fear; it is the anticipation of something ominous which takes you out of your comfort zone. When actually engulfed in the unfamiliar situation of any kind - whether people, places, circumstances or events - the threat is reduced.

The anticipation of a potential threat can actually give you sleepless nights. As long as the threat is yet to materialize, it can be disturbing. However, once in the midst of the dreaded situation, you are surprised at how relatively easy it is to cope with it. Take the example of tentatively putting a finger in freezing water: once immersed, you may actually enjoy the cold sensation. Besides, the energy of the force of cold also compensates. By being aware and adapting to situations, the impact is not so unbearable.

The spiritual path is similar. Going through all the conditioning is an ongoing journey where you explore and experience aspects of yourself. You learn to let go of those things you have accumulated that are not good for you. Letting go is one of the hardest things in life. How can I learn to let go? Letting go of ego, fear, confusion, attachment is very difficult. Yet it has to be done. Once you let go, you are free and the burden is gone.

Consider this: fulfilling an obligation, such as a duty or a debt, can give tremendous relief. You know that sooner or later you have to pay what you owe, no matter whether in cash or kind; there is no escape. Is it not much easier to accept the debt and pay up with happiness? It also removes the threat of consequences if you were to default.

The possibility of getting stuck is greater and full of suffering: you need to proceed, grow out of all that conditioning and move on. Even people concerned with spiritual growth get stuck. This is a long journey and the reward of it is the journey itself. Another concept is that one day - some day in the future - you will be rewarded. This is not so; the reward is ongoing, constantly. You are simply not aware of the reward. The reward of any action comes instantly and the whole journey becomes very fulfilling. It is good to apply chameleon-like qualities to merge into the prevailing environment.

This journey is a good example of how you can accept things and overcome your own fear and anxieties. Confronting others is the second phase of life, but overcoming and facing your own self, your fears, insecurities and complexes has to come first. Once you overcome those then you can face the world. You have worked out your problems and that is the meaning of the journey, as your path will lead to enlightenment.

While everyone is potentially divine, darkness is also part of oneself. Once you recognize your divinity, your journey becomes smooth. Of course some religions and cultures have a problem accepting that.

If you were to claim that you are divine, even today such statement could sentence you at least to ridicule or worse, you could incur the wrath of the 'righteous' condemning you to death. Take the example of Socrates: as he was given the life sentence of drinking the hemlock, his statement was: "I wonder who people will remember more in the future, you or me?" Even in the twenty-first century you are not safe with such a claim.

The world generally welcomes ignorance. No one wants you to really think, to be wise and enlightened. When you are dull or disinterested and under the control of the government and the politicians, that implies that you follow the dictates of your government system, social norms or leaders, you do not oppose anything and you do not bother anyone.

Instead, you should know the truth and not to be affected by anyone. Such is the spiritual world. In the material world, the more ignorant you are, the better it is for everyone. You have to choose: do you want to be enlightened or remain ignorant the whole life where you can be manipulated to your disadvantage?

Chapter

20 There are Many Paths

There are many paths, many roads and trails. Some paths are very beautiful and fulfilling: other paths can be roads of misery, full of thorns and disease where you receive a very bumpy ride. The choice is yours whether you want to take the path of beautiful scenery and uplifting vibrations or if you want to take the difficult thorny path. Life presents us with many choices. While not all the choices can be controlled by your own desires, all wishes and desires you create will become part of your personality and/or consciousness. In some way or other you have to go through them eventually, it is just a question of time. Such is the power of the psyche: whatever you create you will have to experience although the timeline may vary. What you may wish for today may not happen now but can manifest much later. The problem is that later you may have outgrown your original desire; you do not want it any more. Well, that is too bad, because then you will have to take it. There is no way out, as was demonstrated in the story of Krishna and the Thief.*

You are so eager when you want something. The mind is very tricky and complex. For example, walking through the market you may want to have what you see. The mind is like a child always wanting, now chocolate then ice cream and later a toy. When you are a child you may want all the small toys. That does not change much later; when you are older, your selection of toys changes accordingly. Then you think that you are grown up, but you are not really; you still want. The only difference is that now the toys are bigger and more expensive. It is the nature of the immature mind that it wants to acquire ever more, identifying with objects or possessions, whether car, house, brand or appearance.

There are many different paths to choose and many crossroads to negotiate. Some roads become dead ends - you see the sign: 'Road Closed' - whereas other roads circle back on themselves, bringing you back to where you began. Life is like that. You keep going around life, experiencing all, like going to work, growing a garden, getting married, having different professions, and then, after twenty or thirty years, you feel that you have been going round in circles. You pause and ponder: where am I? You have forgotten where you are and who you are and you wonder where you have to go next. So where do you go: same old places, New York, Bangkok, Bombay, Paris, Los Angeles - all the same old places of the world. You have been on a merry-go-round, getting nowhere. It is a round world and you can only go round.

The world is not infinite, infinity is beyond the world. I spoke to you about the blind man in a big building with eighty-four apartments and only one exit. He goes round and round, then misses the exit and he has to start again. In some way you could consider this as getting lost, yet at the same time it can become a passage of discovery. Rather than feeling lost, consider it a sightseeing tour.**

Yet it is part of life too that when you do not expect anything, things may happen. Many times you may look for something in vain, yet quite unexpectedly you may stumble upon it.

You may have seen a bull or donkey grinding corn by going around the wheel with blinkers on a harness. He may be going the whole day, round and round, maybe thinking that he is on a big journey.

It can be the same with people, closing their eyes, walking miles and doing the same things over and over again, yet remaining at the same spot, getting nowhere. It is reminiscent of the adage: 'I don't know where I am going, but I'm making jolly good time'.

There is no question that there are many paths, the point is you need to consider how wisely you select your path - the road towards your destination, towards your fulfillment of life's destiny. The choice is yours. Much depends on the way you have accepted life and programmed yourself. Your total unfoldment manifests according to the way you have conditioned your mind. If you look at the overall picture of your life, you come to know that a certain amount of your life is predestined. Many things are not in your hands. However, you do have complete control over other things. Similarly, within your house, you have control over the internal maintenance design standards, whereas any external changes are subject to external regulations. The issue is whether you have managed wisely those things over which you do have control.

Life consists of many aspects. We have spoken of the gunas, the qualities of sattva, rajas and tamas, the positive, the active and the negative tendencies. You cannot avoid them; they are with you daily. How you handle those qualities is entirely in your hands. As I have said, you can compare this situation to maintaining a house. If you do not make the effort to maintain the house, to keep it in good condition, it will deteriorate and finally collapse. You need to make an effort to keep up your responsibilities, given the general tendency of inertia (tamas) in the physical world. Just as you need to make an effort to maintain your house, so you should maintain your physical body and your spiritual well-being.

You can condition your mind to be either negative or positive, starting with the food you eat. It takes little effort and time to prepare fresh and healthy food. Unfortunately it may even be more convenient to get prepared processed food which pollutes your body and can affect your mind.

How many emotions are created in ignorance? You may have done everything right as far as you know, then suddenly you are confronted with some unpleasant 'drama' and you wonder what you have done to deserve this. You may not have done anything to contribute to such an event, yet you have to go through it with all the resulting emotion and commotion. However, if you are a person of balance, you become an observer and do not participate in the ongoing drama around or within you. You just watch it unfold, without your participation. The poet mystic Kabir says: "I am going through the market, but I am not a buyer". You do not have to participate in any drama that is taking place around you or within you, you can detach yourself. One can recall the example of "The Buddha's Gift". ***

You are not obligated to participate in another's crisis, problems or drama. You can give advice - if needed or asked for - once, and then leave it alone. It does not help to become involved, rather you are perpetuating the drama. It also does not help to react to a perceived insult, rather it multiplies the conflict. You are not assisting anyone. If someone is sick and you go to visit, it does not improve anything to tell that you have also been sick. It is your option to participate or not. You can decide not to become engaged in any conflicts or quarrels.

You follow your path of positivity which will lead you to fulfillment. Your external path may be somewhat limited, but your inner, spiritual journey is infinite. When you make a journey in the world, this is limited, finite. The inner journey, however, is infinite. Your body may be connected with the world, but your Self is connected with the Infinite, which is endless.

We have previously spoken about finding the 'Technique to Live'. The most valuable gift is the gift of knowledge. What can be better than a blueprint on how best to live your life? It gives you optimum advantage, provided that you integrate such knowledge along the way. You should not have regrets at the end of your days. It is important at the end of your life to be able to review it with sincerity:

- I have lived well;
- I have no regrets; and
- I have opened every door available to me.

It is important to conclude with true understanding: I have done everything possible to make my life happy and fulfilled.

* See: "But Guruji" "The Truth Will Set You Free".

** See: "The Human Gift" - chapter 25

*** See: "Renewal of Happiness" - chapter 13, "Enjoying the Beauty" - chapter 17.

Chapter

21 Transforming Your Senses

People can read, write, think, hear and talk a lot, yet time and again fail to implement or experience what has been learned. That seems to be the most difficult task. What you understand and what you are convinced of has been programmed into your system for such a long time that it is very difficult to change. There is highly entertaining, fascinating, even intoxicating mystical and mysterious knowledge. Yet when it comes to following it in your daily lives that special knowledge vanishes like a puff of smoke.

The influences of the outside world are generally so strong that the effect of a weekend seminar does not seem to last very long - especially when dealing with the negative/tamasic forces. The real benefit only becomes apparent when you are able to put into practice what you have learned. Suppose you have a problem with A why would you want to talk to B or C? Rather, deal with the person your problem is related to. Unfortunately human nature gets in the way and you forget the teaching. So much knowledge is available, yet very little is absorbed or understood.

People request frequently that more Teachers should come to teach and be available - why? You already have more teaching than you deserve or have been able to handle so far - less than one percent has been grasped. If you cannot carry a weight of ten kilos, how will you manage to carry a hundred kilos?

Sometimes it happens that you are chosen - selected for some greater task - but you do not understand your task because you get confused. You do not understand that you have been selected for a higher purpose, some special mission. As you do not understand, the great opportunity that may be coming to you will pass you by. This unique opportunity is lost because you cannot appreciate or value it.

That is why I said: prepare! Do not bother about finding a Teacher or Master. It is the Teacher who will find you after due preparation - as it was in the case of Narendra (later to become Svami Vivekananda). The only thing you can do is to prepare in humility. When you are ready, prepared and selected for the great purpose you are very fortunate. But actually, preparation - sadhana - is the main thing for any work.

The real student will do his homework, will make the effort to study and become familiar with the subject and be prepared. If you are lazy, you do not want to read or study, but you want to pass the exam anyhow. How can that happen, how can you get a degree without having the knowledge?

It will only work when you are ready and prepared. So much knowledge has been given throughout history. You have been given so many tools, techniques, helpful instructions and examples, so many keys. Yet you keep forgetting the right key. You may lose the keys and then you cannot open the right door. You become confused, disillusioned and after ten or more years you ask the same questions.

Dealing with human complexities is not easy. Humans are expert in complicating the simplest thing, creating conflict, drama and crisis, even war - there is a plethora of dramas, crises and problems, but for what purpose? Where is the real problem? Life should be happy and joyful. The problem lies in your perception and understanding. Everything is energy; money, thought, speech, your gifts to others, sexual force - all is energy. But humanity does not understand the real meaning of energy. In the classic philosophy of India three categories are described: Yantra, Mantra and Tantra:

- Yantra represents many symbols in the form of diagrams, explaining the mystery of the cosmos in symbolic forms - each diagram dealing with a different aspect.
- Mantra is the mystical power in seed form - invoking the various energies from minute to vast through sound and vibration. Its power is immense - invoking inner cosmic energy, the underlying powerful energy - and bringing that energy out. There are millions of mantras, developed and applied, according to individual development and growth.
- Tantra is the most complex category. There are many aspects of tantric yoga - the sexual aspect is just one aspect of Tantra. Tantric yoga encompasses the Shiva and Shakti principle - Purusha, the male principle and Prakriti, its female counterpart. Everyone is a combination of this Shiva/Shakti principle. Recognize that principle: sexual energy can help you understand and unfold the secret of the Shiva/Shakti principle. Very few people understand this concept, and more to the point, even fewer want to know. Sadly, the only thing people have heard is the name 'Tantra' in its distorted form without having any idea what it actually represents. They do not understand its meaning and what it involves: the mystery of the sacred, perennial and creative principle of all organisms on earth.

Almost all civilizations and religions have denied and prohibited the sexual power as something that should not be mentioned or discussed. The point is you cannot escape it: it is right inside you and it wants to manifest. But then what happens? Everyone is engaged in its practice, yet it is misused and abused, degraded and maligned. People do not appreciate what they are actually dealing with and how to utilize it. One cannot be surprised that under such circumstances the true tantric practices have gone underground. In order to understand such principles you have to evolve yourself.

If two people, a couple, follow the path of Tantra properly they could create tremendous power - enough to create an Evolved Soul in their incarnation. Then even sex can become a divine and spiritual act. Unfortunately it is the body, the physical consciousness, desire and lust which drives people whereas the most beautiful aspect - the door to greater consciousness - is closed. Thus the sexual act remains a physical act.

There are two things that have created disaster in the world: sexual power and monetary power. Time and again throughout history these have been abused by the human being. Apart from the present financial crisis, people also continue to have sexual crises. Humans cannot handle sexual power. Not only is there little understanding, many cultures have denied or demonized sexual power: they categorize it as something that is 'bad' and should not exist. How foolish is that? It rarely occurs to anyone that without sexual power there would be no life; you would not have been born, and you would not exist in your physical body. Yet sex is denied, distorted and corrupted. It has come to the point that if you want to defame anyone, bring someone down, all it needs is to spread the word of sexual misdemeanor, a scandal. That could tarnish the reputation of a public figure instantly. You would think that by now people would be tired of all this, yet the same old corrupt concept persists. Move on and understand the mystery instead.

Each physical pleasure you get through the function of your five senses does not compare to the pleasure you could experience if you were to transform them. That result would be bliss. On the lower level you get sukh-happiness, and then dukh-suffering, pleasure is followed by pain. However when transformed it can result in anandam - bliss, followed by liberation. In ancient India, people were taught how to transform the senses into the higher consciousness. Some temples were built for this purpose, until later they were destroyed by invaders. Thereafter knowledge went underground.

Tantra does not deny your desires; rather it encourages you to grow through them and to understand them. When you can evolve yourself you will come to the point when you no longer fall. You will no longer be trapped by the cycle of pleasure and pain. As long as you are caught on the lowest level of your senses, you will have guilt, regret, repentance, fear, and insecurity. If sex brings you that much suffering it may be a good idea to remain celibate and safe. Do not go near the fire if it burns you. If you want to be slim and healthy, do not indulge in overeating to satisfy your very physical senses. It is a human tragedy that you want to indulge your senses, yet you also want to disavow the responsibility; it is much easier to place blame. At times the blaming game can go to absurd extremes, as seen frequently in modern litigation. Make up your mind what you want.

The idea is to live your life free from guilt, fear, insecurity and crisis. Why would you want to do something that will create a crisis or problem? No one forces you. Take a good look at your motivation: what prompts you, what makes you do anything? Actually, what you do or not do is of no importance really; your motivation is the deciding factor! That seems to be the biggest problem for humans, to deal with the five senses in the right way. At times human actions resemble a spider weaving its web and getting caught in that same web.

Only true knowledge will show you the way out of this dilemma. Guided by knowledge everything you do will be pure and sacred. In India it is a custom that before eating, the food is offered to the Divine: "it is all Yours and I am taking it as prashad - a blessed gift". As such it becomes a sacred act.

Similarly, everything that you do, can become part of your sadhana when offered as a token to the Divine. Thus your acts grow through you and you grow through your acts. When walking, feel that you are walking towards the Divine. This way every act: walking, talking, eating, speaking, can become an offering and a medium for growth. There will be no crisis, no fear and insecurity since every act is based on the higher principle. Keep your spiritual fire burning in your heart. Do not allow any act of yours to disturb you and upset you. Every act should be contributing to your growth and, when you apply yourself, accordingly you will see the amazing result.

Symbolically, when the student goes to the Teacher, he takes an empty lota -a metal vessel used for drinking, carrying, or drawing water from a well.You say to your Teacher: "This is what I am, an empty vessel; please fill me with your energy and wisdom." You cannot go to the Teacher filled with your old ideas and conditioning to receive the true knowledge; you have to discard the old and familiar habits in order to become an empty vessel to receive. You have to empty body, mind and senses and be ready to receive the energy of joy and bliss, so that you can live your life to the fullest. Then there will be no regret, no guilt and no insecurity because you know that you carry the great spiritual strength and you have nothing to fear. My advice to you all is: prepare.

The aspect of the Shiva/Shakti principle is within each and every one of you. Chanting the mantra: 'Om Namo Shivaya' - will bring that aspect into manifestation. It is part of you, but you do not know that. You do not know that you are missing a great treasure. That is why the Master has to see if you are ready or not. You cannot give such energy prematurely; when energy is given you have to be ready.Even if I were to give you such great energy, you would not be able to hold or understand it. It is very important to preparè yourself so that you can be ready. That work is in your hands alone.

In the meantime treasure what you have, appreciate and be happy with yourself. Do not create crises, guilt and insecurity, do not make yourself unhappy. You have every reason to be happy; you have been given so much and there is every reason to be grateful, to enjoy life and to bring fulfillment into your life. Do not get caught in the small things of your life. Remember that you are in control, not governed by your doubt and insecurities. You have total freedom; you are in control of our own destiny and of your own life. No one can influence you to do what you do not want to do. Live for the higher purpose. Do not devalue or lower the precious gift you have been given through undignified thoughts and acts. When you can see the Light and Love in everything you do, you will see how you are transformed.

Chapter

22 Sunrise – Sunset

Many times I have reminded people that when looking for answers to numerous daily problems, Mother Nature is a wonderful teacher. Most of the lessons you need for living happily and contentedly can be found in nature. Look at the example of birds. In the evening when the Sun goes down and night draws in, birds will end their song, their flights and their gathering; all activities become suspended. Birds will fly home to their nests at night and tuck their heads under their wings. When morning comes there is a joyful awakening with active twittering and delightful song. Then, as the Sun rises, all busy activities will commence once again.

The human being should emulate that: when you awaken both mind and body are ready for truly creative work whereas in the evening your mind should begin to relax, choosing such activities that will promote serenity and calm. Your mind and your body should go to rest just like our feathered little friends.

There is a constant process of awakening and withdrawing. The rising Sun becomes the symbol of expansion and creative work, whereas the setting Sun represents the sign of withdrawing and resting. This is also the appropriate time for the mind and for the physical body's organs to prepare for rest. It is a time for going deeper into the Self, becoming more peaceful and relaxed, thereby gaining control of body, mind and senses.

Ignoring these natural tendencies by eating heavy food, having stimulating discussions or activities late at night, you may find yourself anxious, irritable and tense at bedtime, with all kinds of thoughts and ruminations attacking you when you are actually looking for restful sleep.Such activities will turn the whole lifecycle upside down.

You know that you have three major levels of consciousness:

- wakeful consciousness;
- sub consciousness; and
- unconsciousness.

Whichever type of consciousness you are in, the other two do not seem to exist. How do you know which consciousness is real? You experience all three levels in twenty-four hours - every day - and how do you know which one is true? Sometimes what you think is not important in a dream maybe even be most important. When you are in the state of sub-consciousness like in a dream, you do not want to stop dreaming, especially if it is a beautiful dream. Waking up you may want to go back into that lovely dream and are not able to. Yet that dream was real to you. Each stage of mind is equally important.

Human beings have two aspects, the external (bahirang) and the internal (antarang). Few people seem to realize the predominant importance of the internal aspect. For when your internal aspect is strong and stable, this will also reflect in your external life, just as a disturbed internal aspect will equally affect the external manifestation.

If you spend most of your time focused on externals you will have no time to nurture your internal being. Naturally you cannot ignore your external environment; it is there for you to learn from and to cope with. But I cannot emphasize enough how important it is to balance both aspects. When you do not know how these principles work, you can get involved in wrong activities such as watching disturbing TV at night, whether fictional or news reports. Taking such vibrations into your sleep, it is hardly surprising that this will result in a disturbed and restless night.

When you observe muddy water that has been stirred, this offers a good analogy of how, after it is allowed to rest, it will settle down. Mind is like that. When your thoughts can settle, then all will become much clearer - instead of mind being fueled by muddy, disturbed and confused thoughts.

The physical body is equally disturbed at night if your evening food intake is large and difficult to digest. All bodily organs become less active in the night. Heavy food creates a strain on your digestive system and on the entire body and again, your sleep will be disturbed with tossing and turning while your mind is running wild. This applies especially to the not so young any more. The younger body has more resilience and can cope with more stress than the more mature body. Remember: heavy food is for the day.

Essentially, the physical system is as perfect as the mental system. Yet instead of creating harmony within yourself, you can actually provoke your system into creating chaos, resulting in all sorts of troubles, ailments and diseases. Instead, try to follow the natural laws of harmony and your body, mind and senses will thank you.

The important point is for you to learn how to balance both systems to create harmony. Only you can do this, no one else can bring balance to your system. That is why true knowledge is so important and true knowledge can only be given by the true Teacher. Having a true Teacher to impart the right knowledge - combined with your willingness to implement this knowledge - will help you avoid many struggles and pitfalls in life.

It is said that when you move one step, the Spiritual Master or Teacher will move a thousand steps towards you - as is so expressively explained in the story of "Vishnu and his Devotees" *

However, when you go backwards, the Master will simply sit and wait; He will not run after you, but await your coming to your senses. But then again, if you were to take just one single step, He will take many steps towards you. Few people are aware of the endless dividends you can thus receive.

The whole system - physical, mental, psychological and psychical - needs to be in balance and only you can bring about this balance. Although there may be a tendency to blame others and different situations such as your upbringing, primarily you have to blame yourself. Unless you are truly mentally disturbed, the responsibility of balancing your system lies with you. The faculty of thinking has been given to you as a human being, but if you do not develop and use that gift, it is again your fault. Would a craftsman ignore the many precious tools he has? When you can contemplate and meditate regularly, you can develop that sense of discrimination of what is what, what is helpful and what is a hindrance. Just look at nature, everything seems to work so perfectly; all is in balance if you can truly observe. In spite of all the technological advancements human nature still depends on the natural elements.

Just look at some of the events: snow, rain, floods, droughts, volcanic eruptions and earthquakes; human beings will never be able to defeat or conquer Mother Nature, they can only be her friend. When you understand Mother Nature you can begin to understand yourselves. In the Vedic Age the five elements (Earth, Water, Fire, Air and Sky) were considered most important - given by the Grace of God.

Therefore, understanding of mind, understanding of your lives with the implementation of that knowledge, is very important. Focusing internally will help you understand. A good idea to practice before going to sleep is to chant a mantra, followed by some meditation before going into silence.

* See: "The Truth Will Set You Free" : Maya's Play

Chapter

23 Balancing Sun and Moon

Time keeping in the world has been divided into two systems: the lunar cycles and the solar cycles. The most ancient time keeping was related to the waxing and waning phases of the Moon: fourteen days of brightness and fourteen days of darkness. Two sets of fourteen days form one lunar month of twenty-eight days. In Sanskrit the full Moon is called Chandrama and the Moon is considered to be female. Surya, the Sun, is considered male, and in contrast to the natural lunar time-keeping cycles, a man-made solar calendar has been created. Indian calendars generally adhere to the more accurate lunar cycles, although this does not always translate to the modern way of observing the seasons. Since ancient times the lunar calendar has been regarded as an infallible way of counting time.

In relation to the earth the body of the Sun is far, whereas the Moon is relatively near. Sun is the pivotal point around which the earth rotates, yet the protective Moon circles the earth, thereby acting as shield from an overexposure of Sun rays by blocking out the fierce light and heat at intervals. It is the Moon that balances the heat from the furnance of the Sun. The Sun alone would cause such dehydration that the earth would simply disappear. Moon is the big balancer of our planet earth. People take the Moon lightly without recognizing its real importance. Although the Moon and the earth are far from each other (250,000 miles) they are interdependent. It is important to remember that all life is interdependent.

Look at the physical body's interdependency with the subtle body: with mind, intellect, ego and emotion. All are codependent and they all interact in this symbiotic relationship. Yet the ego of the subtle body likes to rule supremely. It will sacrifice its subtle body partners and in extremes even forfeit the physical body to get its way, just to be right. Not knowing any better, ego is mainly used by the ignorant in all manners of competition with others: my body, my house, my car, my achievement, my success. What is this, but merely a childish way of showing off? Look at the rivalry between neighbours, prying into each other's business, each wanting to outdo the other. It seems that neighbourly relations are very strange throughout the world. Depending on the kind of neighbours you have, your life may be peaceful - or it can be torture. Today there is such intolerance and lack of consideration towards one's neighbour that in extreme cases this can result in war - both interpersonally as well as internationally.

Moses felt compelled to bring the Ten Commandments to his unruly flock. But look at these rules: these are simple social rules, common sense rules that should not require divine directives. The necessity of such simple rules indicates the low state of consciousness of the people. Moses must have had a lot of trouble with his flock; therefore he stated these commandments as directives from God. Breaking these commandments could incur serious punishment. Is God really so primitive as to create something so commonplace? Would you not expect something truly profound as a divine edict? Do you really need to have divine directions on how to behave? Apparently so, especially since something proclaimed in the name of God is being taken more seriously.

Whenever the name of authority is used it creates more impact. That kind of 'namedropping' is used very widely, usurping the power of some authority. It is not unusual to hear the statement "God wants me to do this, it is His command." Does that mean that that person is a close friend of God and speaks only to him? This is blatant misuse of divine authority based on nothing but ego. Ego can only be paraded in front of someone inferior. The flagrant display of ego in all areas is very apparent as soon as there is a bit more success, a little more money, a little more recognition, power or goods. The naked dance of ego - in unashamed exhibitionism - is always present throughout the world. The world around you judges you by what you have, not what you are. That kind of imbalance can only lead to disaster.

The real spiritual Yogi, the Realized Being, does not have ego since He knows He has all the power: An example during the time of the British occupation of India tells of a Yogi traveling on the train in first class. Usually first class was only reserved for the British. The conductor was moving through the train checking the tickets. Our Yogi smilingly offered him not just one, but several first class tickets. The conductor became very angry and in short order threw the Yogi out of the train. There was the Yogi, just standing on the platform, smiling gently - and the train could not move.

It is a pity that the ego of demeaning another is so prevalent all over world. Happily there are some exceptions, sometimes even found in prominent positions of the world. Such people can create some balance in the otherwise egocentric world.

A famous Sanskrit stanza looks at the human ego-sickness: "You fool, you pride yourself on something so ridiculous, yet you miss what you really have (atma). You live in total ignorance about that which is truly worth knowing." Knowledge about your own atma, the Ultimate Reality, is the most important knowledge, all else is just information.

There is a story about the plight of King Janak's disturbing dream of being destitute in the jungle, yet on awakening in his luxurious palace he wanted to know which reality was the correct one: the dream of suffering or the waking reality within the palace. When seeking an answer from the most 'learned' men in the land he was finally admonished by Sage Ashtavakra on the futility of claiming ownership of land and might. When Janak finally asked what was left that he could offer as a gift, he was told that there was only one thing to give up: the ego of claiming power and possessions. Once he was able do that, the answer would become clear.

As long as you cling to your ego, ego will dictate and rule you. Only when you can go beyond your ego, asking in the true sense: 'who am I?' Will you have clarity.

There is a beautiful tale about Draupadi being humiliated by a demon in open assembly. He attempted to disrobe her. She tried to defend herself by holding on to her sari but her strength was nothing compared to the villain Dushasana'sattempt of removing the sari. Draupadi felt totally helpless although her Grand Protector Bhisma, the Guardian of the Clan and her five powerful husbands were present, they were unable to protect her, nor was she able to protect herself. Only when she sought divine intervention could she be saved. In her extreme distress she called on Krishna. Krishna appeared and it is said that while the sari was being pulled off her by the demon, the sari never finished - until the demon was exhausted!

The question arises: why did Krishna not come before allowing her to reach this level of humiliation? At first Draupadi thought that her human assistants would come to her aid. Finally, when she realized that help was not forthcoming, she called on Krishna. He appeared and rescued her and she was saved.

The point is that when you take matters into your own hands you have to manage yourself and you are responsible. You may look for help here and there and you may be disappointed, but it makes you responsible. As long as you cling to your own ego you will have to manage yourself - until you let go of your ego when divine intervention can manifest.

Like Sun and Moon interact to create a healthy balance that allows life to flourish on earth, you need to bring balance within your own Sun and Moon. You have heard the saying: as above, so below; consider the powerful Sun as the Ultimate Reality and the Moon as a moderator and transformer, reflecting the Sun's rays into your consciousness, balancing your life.

Balancing Moon and Sun is necessary. It will help to meditate on the sun in the daytime and to contemplate the qualities of the Moon at night.

Chapter 24

Connections

Today is a rainy and windy day. We have all experienced rainy and windy days. Does that mean that a rainy or stormy day is a bad day? Not at all, it is simply a wet and windy day, no more and no less. Have you ever tried to tune to that kind of energy, to have an awareness of - and a connection to - the wind element? At the next opportunity try to focus and attune to that wind energy, try to connect with the wind. It can be an interesting experience.

Connection to that which is healthy, uplifting and life-enhancing is not always easy. A prevailing attitude is: if all is well then I will be happy. You forget that you carry your happiness and love with you at all times; the great joy and knowledge that is within you. Then why do you feel so unhappy, so miserable and so lost? In a way you are like a beggar sitting on a treasure, yet there he sits begging for pennies. He sits there the whole life feeling sad, poor, and miserable and then he dies. The people come to take him to be cremated and only later, when others try to gather his belongings, there, under the old mattress the beggar had been sitting on, they find a diamond. Yet the whole life this beggar was needy, depending on the alms of others. He had been a rich man yet he lived a very poor life. He did not realize the wealth he had all along.

Similarly, you are the symbol of great joy and fulfillment. If that were not the case, you would not be alive. You are a spark of that light which sustains the universe, the same energy which sustains the stars, the Sun, the Moon and the entire cosmos.

That energy is yours, yet you are lost in your own negativities such as ego, arrogance and confusion and desires. It is very hard to remind yourself. At times you might say: "I don't feel like doing this, that or the other". Yet when it comes to your own ultimate happiness and joy you have to be active. You have to seek it and you have to find it. Connect yourself to that thought. It means that every day on awakening you look forward to the great unfoldment. Say: "Today is going to be a fulfilling day for me, a day of new and inspiring knowledge, saswath, and every day the joy is new." If your day is saswath, perennially intoxicating and new and joyful, how come you become so depressed? Remember: the whole world is made of the three gunas, the three subtle qualities of satva, rajas and tamas. When you make the statement that you do not 'feel like' doing something positive or uplifting, that statement reflects your current state of mind - either rajas or tamas - within the collective consciousness of whatever environment you happen to find yourself in.

Whether this is a positive or negative environment, you are making a statement of your current collective environment, the one you have connected yourself to. The collective consciousness of any particular environment cannot be high; it is the individual consciousness which has the potential of being high.

Collective consciousness varies; for instance, when you have political elections, you may like a certain candidate, identify with the 'goals' of that particular candidate, which means you are no longer just you. Because you have connected to the vibrations of that candidate - if he wins you are happy, if he loses, you are upset - you can no longer maintain your individual consciousness. Instead, since you have allowed this to happen, you have become a part of the collective consciousness. Remember that it is you who allows your senses to connect with a prevailing energy. Ultimately it is in your own hand where you chose to connect and what energy you receive. For instance, were you aware of the wind energy today? Or were you sitting in silence not quite knowing what to do? Connecting to the power of the wind you may have experienced the manifestation of the wind. You can try to harness that prevailing energy into your life.

In this popular predominantly material world there are so many things going on: politics, football, games of any kind, so-called celebrities and many more. All seem to have fan clubs. My question to you is: what does it mean to you when you connect yourself to any of these people or their activities? Actually it profits you nothing, the result is zero and yet the whole world is hooked into this; you buy magazines, read all the gossip, buy photos, medallions, even so called religious paraphernalia. It is all centered around different personalities, whether religious, political or from the entertainment industry. Do tell me: what do you benefit?

There are exceptions however: if you meet someone who has done outstanding work or that person is able to inspire you to change your life positively. Otherwise, what does it mean if some prominent person comes to your town and everyone flocks around that person in some kind of admiration? It is entertainment and nothing else. Well, there may be a material benefit of some kind for some, but spiritually such situations can only impoverish you. You may want to support all kind of causes or leaders, yet eventually, if you really think about it, this contributes nothing to your own real happiness for it is nothing more than transitory entertainment. However, if you connect yourself to someone who has brought about some wonderful achievement in a spiritual sense, or even in the real sense without the expectation of monetary reward, that at least can have some benefit. Essentially I am not talking about achievement in the material sense, rather attainment in the perennial sense, the lasting sense that reflects to what extent you have been inspired. How far are you connected to that and to what extent has this knowledge been translated into your individual life? Your happiness is the most important point.

Only if you are happy or content can you make another happy. By being unhappy you cannot help yourself, leave alone the whole world.

To fulfill the concept of individual growth some people have given up everything and retreated to remote mountain peaks to achieve self-realization. Sometimes others, less aware, may call such people selfish, yet unless you first know the fullness of all knowledge, how can you help or inspire anyone else? Those who are confused and unhappy will never be able to help others. Only those who are clear in their own mind and perception, in their understanding of their own lives, these are the ones who will make a difference.

In any case, spirituality is a state of mind. Unfortunately much energy is lost in desire. Statements like: 'I feel like - or I don't feel like doing this that and the other' you cannot afford. Time is running. Every day you may wake up and think: 'I don't feel like doing spiritual practices.' Fine, so let time run by and who knows when you will have a second chance?

All creatures have a sense of love and compassion that is inbuilt. Not only humans have this sense of love and care; all creatures have that quality. By interacting and creating a bond with any animal you will see this inbuilt quality. This has not been learned in any school, yet animals know exactly how to express themselves. All creatures have a sense of caring toward their offspring, you can call it love or compassion, joy and happiness; essentially it is an inbuilt quality.

In addition to this, humans have been given thinking power and a sense of discrimination. But if this thinking power is not being used in contemplation and meditation, you actually fall below the conduct of other creatures. Animals follow their instinct and do everything instinctively. Human beings have intuition and instinct but if you do not use your intuition, how can you even be compared to the animal, which has often more discipline.

It can be said that humans have a quest: they do think about life, death, and happiness; they think about death and birth, they think about love, but what do they do about it? It is alright to think about all this, but what are you doing about that contemplation? The majority of people float like a small wave on the water subject to wherever the wind carries them - they float in the world, subject to their current environment. The three gunas fluctuate constantly. One's individual duty is not to get lost, lost in desire. In the long run no money, no house, no fancy car or name and fame will help when you are desperate. Then what will save you? Are you doing enough to achieve real fulfillment? What is important to you? Many times I inspire people to have satsang. Fine, one satsang, maybe two and then the enthusiasm fades. There is no consistency. How can you get tired of truth, of love and of happiness? One should never tire of those wonderful qualities.

Many things are not right in this world, but you cannot change it; what can you do as an individual? Although this is such a confused world, you have your own power; you have your individual power. Since you cannot change the world, how can you change anyone - unless that person wants to be changed? Many people have practiced negativity for decades; the whole life has been engaged in negativity. The American constitution correctly states that the pursuit of happiness is your constitutional right. The pursuit of happiness is also a universal law; it is your birthright. Yet often people seem to practice the pursuit of unhappiness; maybe they have a mission to destroy, to hate, to attack, or to defame others.

Often the two major tools to distort and to confuse are money and sex. That scenario has grown totally out of control. Most religions, whether Christianity, Islam or Judaism have a condemning view of sex. How can you condemn sex when this is the very principle upon which life starts? The philosophy of Tantra, which hardly anyone understands in the modern world, is actually the philosophy of life, of understanding creation. That is why in India the Shiva Lingam has a highly symbolic meaning - Shiva and Shakti. The beautiful philosophy of creation has been repeatedly and deliberately distorted, demeaned, abused and confused. Human beings have been in the habit to use money and sex as a tool to destroy each other, because humanity has not understood the meaning of either. Both money and sex are energies, yet the entire world has failed in its understanding of the value of sex and of money. The so-called sophisticated society today is really the least sophisticated or civilized.

People have a lot to learn. We still have wars, still have poverty and still have disease. This is not a golden age, it is a different world: it is the world of maya, illusion. Consider what people do to each other, thereby also creating and reaping the consequences of their deeds in the illusion of this universe. Have you examined what illusion is? It is something that is not true, does not exist, a mirage. Illusion is that there is death, but you do not remember it. Illusion is that you think something is yours, yet nothing is yours; your ego and your desires are your illusion. The entire world you have created for yourself is an illusion. Finally, what is left that is yours and that can go with you? Your own consciousness, that is all.

People often cling to those illusions and identify with them. Look at the many marriages throughout the world, the majority are often fake, there is nothing real, it is a mere convenient arrangement of living together. Marriages are not made in heaven and this is keenly realized when you have to live and maintain this 'marriage' here on earth. Let us, of course, not demean the significance of marriage in its most positive form.

Love is like a spring, constantly renewing itself. It is a never ending energy. Can you maintain such love? For that you must evolve. Only when you reach a higher level of consciousness will you know what love actually is - and you will know your individual path.

For instance, Jesus said: 'You want me to die? Alright I will die.' He knew His fate and knew exactly what He was doing. His supposed utterance and frequently quoted phrase, beseeching God "Why hast Thou forsaken Me?" is totally contradictory to the divinity of Jesus. He was not a fool, not confused; He knew exactly what path He had taken, and it was His choice. Only fools don't know. The truly wise person knows exactly where the road is leading. He will only walk it when He knows the destination.

Likewise, why should you be confused? You are here in this world to be happy and to love. If you do not know how to do it, you have to learn to love and to be happy. That is why the teachings are being given. That is why the Divine Manifestation occurs from time to time and place to place.

Love is yours but you are not aware of it; it is like a dormant energy. Dormant energy is like fire, you pile up the wood and light the fire, and when the wood is all burnt up it seems that the fire is out. Not so, for below the ashes is still the dormant, glowing heat which can be rekindled. Likewise, both love and eternal life are dormant within you. You need to become aware of that. Time and again you have been told that and therefore, the statement 'I don't feel like meditating or loving any more' is simply a thought that will pull you down. How can you have exposed yourself to the Highest and removed yourself from that energy? You can liken this to a day of bright sunshine, yet you sit in the house with closed doors and windows; you get no sunlight and no fresh air. The Sun does not stop shining because your house is closed. Fresh air will not stop because you closed your windows. Each time you close doors and windows to the highest energy, you fall back. It is your job to keep the window open. This is your endeavor, your karma yoga. Do not get lost in your own little desires and ego, thereby getting caught into your own very small world. You have to create the beautiful world within you. That world is there for you and it is within your reach.

If you allow yourself to be influenced by the fluctuations of the gunas, like those of the market forces, you will be just as unstable, happy one moment, miserable the next. If you want to have consistency in your life, you have to create your own individual world. The world may be full of contradictions, but nonetheless it is a beautiful world. Since you are all potentially divine there is no reason why you should not connect yourself to your own divinity.

At the same time be aware of the inherent inertia, the inertia of your ego and procrastination which prevents you from seeing the true light. To enter the atmosphere of higher energy, you have to evolve. To be able to go to the Sun, you have to develop and grow, that you may tolerate the high energy. You have to become Sun-like and shine.

It is not always helpful to give people extra time and attention if they are not ready to receive this energy. It does not benefit someone if that person is not ready, not prepared or evolved enough to understand and appreciate the Grace. In the meantime it is important for you to prepare to achieve everything you can in your life. This is in your hands. Do not wait for others to do it for you; it does not work that way. The only way is for you to prepare and strive to be ready. Then, whatever you may aspire to, you will receive, but you have to be ready.

Sometimes people pretend to be a spiritual person needing help for their own undeclared agenda, yet the play of maya makes it very clear who and what that person is.

It reminds me of a story: A Yogi was sitting in meditation in the forest when a little mouse came by and, jumping with fright, it now sat shivering with fear in the Yogi's lap looking at a big cat sitting right in front of it. The Yogi, in meditation, glanced at the pitiful creature and said: "My little mouse, become a cat". Immediately the mouse became a cat, a big cat ! When the other cat saw the new and bigger cat, he became afraid and ran away. Now the new cat was happy just roaming around in the forest for a few months. After some time, the Yogi was in meditation again, and the cat came to sit next to Him. Suddenly, as the cat looked around, it jumped in shock at the vision of a big dog glaring at it. The Yogi, aroused by the fearful vibrations, opened one eye, saw the dog and the trembling cat and said to the cat: "Alright, little cat, now become a dog". So the cat became a dog, a big and growling one. Seeing the new fierce dog, the other dog put his tail between his legs and ran away. All was well in the forest.

Once again, sometime later, the Yogi was sitting in meditation with the dog peacefully by His side. The dog had been dreaming a little, when suddenly he heard a loud growl. As the Yogi came out of meditation, opening the other eye, the dog was sitting in His lap and shivering with fear while a lion was standing in front of him. "Alright", the Yogi said, "become a lion". And a lion he became. Now our former little mouse roamed the jungle joyously as a lion, not afraid of anything. He enjoyed a wonderful life - until the day another lion saw him and laughed at him; "Ha haha, you are not a real lion, you are not a bit like us, you are just a product of that Yogi."

Now that made the new lion very angry and he thought; 'this is all the fault of that Yogi, He made me a lion and I was enjoying being a lion and now I am being challenged. I shall have to correct this situation. This Yogi has to be eliminated. When no one is looking I will just go and kill Him because as long as the Yogi is there they will all know that I am not a real lion.'

Sneakily the lion approached the meditating Yogi, ready to pounce. Just then the Yogi opened both eyes and seeing the lion attacking Him, just says: "Oh my child, go back to being a mouse." (And that is what happened and it is the end of the story and it was also the end of the mouse - because the other real lion swallowed it in one bite.)

When people come to me with a variety of desires, how can they cope? For instance, any ambition is a potent energy.

How many people can handle that energy? The little story of the mouse becoming a lion illustrates that giving power to those who are not ready is not always a good idea; in fact it can be counterproductive. Instead, try to remember that all those things you do have are resources that are meant to help you. You are not their owner. Do not claim ownership of the blessings that have been given to you. You have every reason to be happy and to pursue the path of happiness. And when you follow the path of happiness, not only will you be happy, but you will also be able to influence others to be happy and humble. For that you have been given ample resources and opportunities. Appreciate the grace and the blessing that is being offered to you with the opportunity to grow and to connect positively.

Chapter

25 The Human Gift

According to Indian astrology everyone has a predominant animal quality, be that dog, cat, lion or mouse: everyone has some quality akin to an animal. For the purpose of arranging a physical marriage in India, traditionally the animal influences of both potential partners are being explored to see if they complement each other.

Animals are most fascinating creatures. We had talked about the twittering of birds, which sometimes resembles communication within a large assembly. Generally birds appear to communicate peacefully, yet there are exceptions. Some birds come across as very aggressive. Have you ever seen a hawk being harassed by crows? The crows will not give up until the hawk flies so high they cannot follow. Look at the interesting facts of migration: small and seemingly delicate creatures flying all day with infallible instinct and strength. It appears that birds have an inbuilt GPS system; all this is done instinctively. It is part of their genetic programming.

Animals do not have minds like humans. You have the ability to think as much as you like with no restriction on any kind of fantasy. That power is given; you can just sit and fantasize about anything, whether you want to be king, or queen, famous or infamous; there is no limit to thought. You can even commit a crime in your thoughts without being punished. In short, whether you have high thoughts or low, kind or mean, there are no boundaries. You can create love, hate, anything you like. The human being is the only one with such a gift, no other creature in the entire cosmos has this gift - and how you use it is up to you. Thought also implies responsibility. You have to remember that even your fantasies can affect your mood, your entire being, including your subsequent actions.

As I said, no other creature in the cosmos has this gift. There are eight million and four hundred thousand types of creatures on this planet alone; all with different characteristics.
Four different categories are considered essential for life to start: humans, animals, plants and rocks - yes, rocks. Depending on your karma and development there is the possibility of having to repeat the entire range of eight million four hundred thousand life forms. Gender can also change, since the soul has no gender, for gender is only part of the body.

I had spoken to you about the analogy of the blind man roaming around in a building with eighty-four doors and being unable to find that door, that human door. The human life is the only life where you can earn karma in the entire cosmos, both good and bad. The human life is the gateway to liberation - in all other life forms you can only spend, you have to complete the term of life allocated, whether dog, cat, mouse, anything and whether on earth or elsewhere. The human life is the only opportunity where you can grow or fall, become liberated and enlightened or condemn yourself.

Before enlightenment you have several choices. You can compare this to a point system, like the airline miles system. You can buy this or that, go to one restaurant or the other, or you save your points for further travel.

Let us say you have accumulated a lot of good karma, having done many good deeds, not having done anything wrong, but you do not have quite enough 'points' for enlightenment. It is said that, when your body dies and you present yourself to the Final Judgment, you are given a choice:

You can either go back as a human to be born into a good spiritual and privileged family that will assist in your further development, or you can go to 'paradise/heaven' to spend all your good karma. There every wish and desire of yours can be fulfilled. However, when you have spent all your 'merit points', back you go to start the whole cycle again.

So you can see that the human life is most precious indeed as the only exit from the cycle of births and deaths. Krishna says in the Bhagavad Gita that there is an exception to the general rule: "When at the time of death you think of Me, you will come to Me".

A little anecdote tells of one man who heard this and thought, 'oh this is excellent; I don't have to exert myself doing good karma as long as I think of Krishna at the moment of death.' So he decided that he would be able to do anything and just enjoy whatever ideas came to him. First he made sure by deciding to give all his children names of divine personalities, like Krishna, Rama, Sita, Gita, and so on. He thought that he could not possibly go wrong since he would be so used to calling the divine names that the divine name would come naturally. He was also a business man and his trade was of great importance to him. Finally the time came when his end was near and he called all his children: Krishna, Rama, Vishnu, Sita, Gita - and as he looked around he saw them all assembled and said: "You idiots, you are all here and who is minding the business?" And then he died.

Unfortunately there are beliefs that when you are young you do not have to think of spirituality now; there will be plenty of time when you are older. First of all, spirituality needs to be in your consciousness - let me give you the example of an Indian sweet, called gulabjamun: bite-sized balls of delicious dough are fried in deep fat, followed by being soaked in sugary syrup. The syrup will soak into the entire confection resulting in a most delicious sweetmeat. Just like the gulabjamun, mind has to soak up spirituality from as early as possible that it may become filled with that kind of 'sweetness'. If you let slip away the opportunity during your younger days, it may be difficult to catch up. Many people in advanced years can become involved in all kind of petty things and being very unhappy. You would expect senior members of society to be wise and more serene, peaceful and calm; unfortunately this is rarely the case.

According to Vedic philosophy human life is divided into four phases, each consisting of twenty-five years: twenty-five years for study and learning the philosophies of spirituality, thereby preparing for later life; then twenty-five years as a householder in marriage and responsibly raising a family by incorporating spiritual principles. This phase is followed by twenty-five years of departure from possessions, withdrawing from external activities, yet taking the role of spiritual mentors and teachers within the family. Finally, the last twenty-five years incorporate the stage of sanyasa, a time of renunciation of all things worldly and withdrawal into contemplation and meditation of the Divine.

Looking at the older generation, how many people are engaged in spiritual matters? The majority are engaged in all kinds of material and entertaining activities, trying to relive their youths, many still looking for chemical sexual enhancements. What kind of consciousness does that reflect? The whole lifestyle is upside down.

Enlightenment is the ultimate achievement of human life, yet people seem to take it very easy. Enlightenment is a life time process and one life may not even be enough. Unless your life has been molded in this way it is very difficult to achieve this consciousness. You have to go through many processes as well as animal instincts.

As I said in the beginning, as a human being you have the gifts of both instinct and intuition, yet for some reason many do not seem to use either. If you used both of these gifts wisely you would be able to handle your life far more easily and simply. In a way animals are better off since they are not corrupted by human folly. Humans are constantly being bombarded by outside developments that hinder using instinct and intuition. You may do something, having been influenced by the media or by friends despite the fact that you know this is not helpful to you. Outside forces, whether food, fashion, language or behaviour are very powerful. These precious gifts of instinct and intuition are given to you to help you uplift and to reach the fullness of your own potential.

Chapter

26 Maintaining Confidence

You may have heard about the practice of 'Ganga Asnan', taking a dip in the Ganga. When people go to Rishikesh dipping into the Ganga will give a feeling of being renewed, uplifted, purified and sanctified. Similarly, most of you have been doing a kind of Ganga Asnan by 'dipping' into the sacred knowledge. It is important to remember the knowledge you have been given and to implement it in your daily life that you may feel the energy and the knowledge continually.

There are two types of knowledge: there is the living knowledge and then there is information knowledge which people carry. The latter is more common. Moreover, those who have a lot of information carry the burden of knowledge if they fail to apply, implement or experience the knowledge of that information. Then there are those who apply true knowledge in their lives, thereby implementing living and fulfilling knowledge. You can only benefit when you implement the true knowledge in your daily lives.

You need to remember the knowledge that has been given, and implement its essence in your daily lives. In addition you need to have a conviction of your own path and carry the confidence that what you are doing is right, what you are practicing is right and good for you - for your body, mind and soul. Do not let anyone confuse you or misguide you, or create doubt within you by all kinds of nasty, negative and offensively demeaning remarks, questioning your commitment to the spiritual path and challenging your new and healthy lifestyle. "Why are you doing this, why are you following this Indian 'thing', why are you following that strange yoga and meditation, that vegetarian diet?" People who say such things are actually only demonstrating their profound ignorance. Anyone of true intelligence would think and inquire, would try to find out before making such comments. No matter how important such people might be within their own field, no matter how many degrees they may have, they are caught in "learned ignorance".

Trying to degrade another's belief and lifestyle without knowing anything about it is called prejudice. Consider the meaning of the term prejudice: judgment before knowledge; the intent to judge something or someone before knowing anything about it - or even trying to find out.

You have to have confidence and know how to reply. For instance you can reply "I do not interfere in and question your drinking and eating habits, in your way of socializing, why do want to bother with mine. You take care of your own life and I do the same."

You have to be strong to respond to people and have confidence in your own beliefs and not to become timid or scared or, worse, to become embarrassed. What are you embarrassed about? Ask yourself.

Those who question and criticize are the ignorant ones; they have not tasted the fruit, they do not know what they are actually missing. On the other hand, you have gone through collective lifestyles and you have moved on; you are engaged in higher pursuit and higher fulfillment. You have left the old habits behind because you found something better.

Some people might say that this or that is not part of their culture, tradition or religion, is not whatever they have normally been able to relate to or identify with. Such people should really examine their statements. For instance, what does it mean that something is not American? America is a land of immigrants and natives with vast cultural differences - so, which one applies? People who make such ignorant statements based on country, race or creed have been the cause of untold suffering in the world, as documented in persecutions and wars.

Truth comes from all sides; if you only want to validate your own limited knowledge, then you cannot claim the Sun, the water or the rain; they do not belong to any one group or nation. People have a habit of making their world very small by being intolerant of anything outside. You can identify with a particular nation or you can identify yourself as a child of Mother Earth instead; she is the Greater Mother of all. However, humans have divided Mother Earth into countless parcels with borders, different languages and limitation of movement for earth's inhabitants. So all is divided, the earth is divided and you are divided, your heart, your mind are divided and the results can be disastrous. Mother Earth is offering you the best and whatever is the best, try to integrate that into your life.

There is a story that illustrates the repercussions of limited vision in the fight for seva, service to the Master. Seva is very important: without seva you cannot 'clean' or purify yourself, as the first stage to receive the knowledge. You cannot come near the great Master. This is the story of such a situation.

One Guru had two disciples. Both disciples wanted to serve the Master, do cooking, washing, cleaning and all the other household chores as seva for the Guru. Unfortunately this did not work out as smoothly as one would have hoped for. These two guru-brothers did not seem to be able to agree on anything and the days were filled with their constant quarreling.

This had been going on for some time and finally the Guru had had enough. "Look here you two, I know you are dedicated and want to do seva, but to quarrel about seva is really not very nice, it is contrary to very spirit of seva. Seva should be done with a happy heart and always in a sense of cooperation, not rivalry or competition. This quarreling has to stop. I have decided to divide the seva - who does what - so that hopefully there will be peace here at the ashram. "

So it was decided down to basic chores: you do breakfast, you do lunch, you do supper, you take care of the laundry, and you clean the rooms; all was divided. Finally all sevas had been allocated. Only one seva was left: who would massage Guruji's feet? Both wanted this special seva. Guruji saw an other argument coming and he said: "Fine, you can each take care of one leg." After some hesitation, that seemed to be agreeable to both disciples.

For some time this arrangement seemed to work smoothly; each man had his particular assigned seva and there was peace - of sorts. The day came, however, that the disciple responsible for the left leg had to go on an errand. In the meantime, the remaining disciple, busy massaging the right foot, saw an opportunity to vent his dislike of his guru-brother, and, finding an iron bar nearby, he gave the left leg a good smack resulting in a huge bruise. Guruji, in meditation at that time, did not really notice very much. However, in short order, the left-leg-disciple returned and seeing what had been done in his absence, became so enraged that when he spotted a hammer nearby, filled with revenge, he let loose on right-leg-disciple's 'seva' . . .

What can you call this example? Torture by disciples? But that is exactly what humans are doing to Mother Earth: we pollute, we abuse, rape and torture our Mother Earth and generally do everything wrong, not concerned about the impact. Pollution travels from one area to another, often affecting pristine protected areas. We may think that someone else is responsible, yet we may have planted the seed, not understanding how pollution travels. We do not realize how interconnected and mutually dependent we are.

It is the small, ignorant mind and mentality that defines 'I and mine' versus 'you and yours'. Remember the old adage:

consider the source, when you hear comments made attacking your positive lifestyle. Do not feel embarrassed or put down, but give them a fitting and very firm reply, for if you do not, you can become a target for further insults and attacks. It has to be set right instantly. Your new lifestyle is something very precious and you cannot allow it to be ridiculed. If another does not have the capability to comprehend the benefits and joy you derive, it does not give them license to deprive you. If someone else cannot enjoy your silence, it does not give them the right to disturb yours.

The belief in yourself that what you are doing is wholesome and right is most important, for if you are filled with insecurities, you can be defeated easily. It is up to you not to allow anyone to confuse you, or to create doubt. When you are sure of yourself people will either love you - or they will leave you alone.

You need to know what is important for your own development, for your own growth and fulfillment. What you are doing is not harming or hurting anyone at all: on the contrary you want to help others by sharing your joy and happiness. It is very important to have confidence in your own convictions.

Take the example of a cow: she crops the grass and transports it half chewed into the rumen, her first stomach, where it is softened and stored. In the second stomach, the reticulum, it is further softened and from there it returns to the mouth to be chewed again in small 'cuds' then swallowed again, and deposited in the third stomach, the omasum, for further processing to be passed finally into the fourth stomach, the abomasum where the actual digestion takes place. Only from here can the nutrients be sent into the system to nourish and energize the body of the cow.

The cow's digestive process is an excellent analogy to the 'digestion' of knowledge for the human being. We hear the message, the teaching, and we might 'ruminate' about its deeper meaning, contemplating further by retrieving the message and mulling things over, just like 'chewing the cud'. Finally we may come to the point of being able to 'absorb' the precious teaching, making it our own and thereby implementing it into our daily lives. It may be helpful to give this cow meditation some thought, and when you see or meet a cow you can consider it a Teacher too.

On that basis, nothing is lost and nothing is wasted; the knowledge implanted is never lost. You may forget for a while, but it is not lost, merely stored in your mental archives. You can use it as you need it. Whenever you focus on the Teacher, the connection is established instantly and the knowledge will come to you.

Remember your teachings and your given tasks and try not to be influenced by negative outer forces, remarks or attitudes. Instead, radiate your positive spiritual energy like a flower radiates fragrance. Walk like a lion, full of confidence and security. A lion needs no confirmation from anyone or anything; he knows exactly who and what he is.

Chapter

27 Initiation

Time and again I have been asked about initiation. There are so many different ideas that there is as much confusion as there are wild concepts about the subject. What is the actual meaning of initiation?

Like anything else initiation has been commercialized. It seems that everyone is giving it and bestowing everyone receiving it with instant 'mastership' and 'guruship'.

In the spiritual marketplace a lot of forces are available, such as in North America: you pay the required amount of dollars and maybe in a few weeks you get a certificate and you can start practicing. That is the tendency in modern times. Almost everything is used, utilized and/or exploited for commercial use.

There are many stages and aspects of initiation. For instance, conception is a form of initiation; birth is a form of initiation and each stage of life presents another form of initiation.

In addition, however, both spiritually and traditionally, initiation has great meaning. Although there are many stages and endless aspects, in the spiritual sense initiation takes place when the Sat Guru imparts the sacred knowledge to the worthy disciple. He initiates you into the path of spirituality. For that matter, when any Teacher decides to give secret knowledge to a disciple or student that is initiation. You could compare spiritual initiation to giving the secret of atomic power to a student. Thus, any secret knowledge, formula, tools or keys imparted to a student to enhance knowledge and understanding regarding the mysteries of life, joy and bliss, is initiation.

Initiation is a course on various levels. Sometimes I am asked what I can offer, what I can give. Well, it is never a question of what I can give, but what and how much you can handle, process and implement. To what extent are you capable of digesting, applying, experiencing, and living the sacred knowledge? Have you purified yourself in body, mind, ego and emotion to be able to handle that kind of powerful energy? I have spoken many times of the subtle body being the transformer for the high spiritual energy to be manifested by the individual. Only once you have purified the subtle body with its four entities: intellect, mind, ego and emotion, will the divine light and knowledge be able to shine through into your consciousness.

Some people are satisfied with little and do not want more responsibility. By way of example, someone may have a salary of five hundred dollars and is satisfied with this. He does not want to handle more, although his possibilities of earning more are endless. I am using this example because people can relate to money. This is a very real example. The same person, when placed in the position that would bring five thousand dollars, does not want that responsibility. Money is also power of a different kind and requires responsibility and wisdom and can equally be misused. The point is: how much knowledge, energy and power can you utilize, handle or integrate for your own balanced growth? I always allow people limitless opportunity to grow and learn mentally and spiritually. The question is: Can you handle it? The sky is the limit. Space is infinite, so is power, so is energy and so is life.

There have been countless examples of humans who were given sudden power. The problem is that when you are given that kind of power and if you are unprepared or your motivation is selfish, there can be misuse, even corruption. History is full of people who were given power and have misused that power: Hitler, Stalin, Napoleon - to name but a few.

The question is always: how do you use such tremendous force or energy? It is for that reason that the true Master will not initiate unless the disciple is prepared and fit for handling this kind of power.

In the area of initiation there is something called shakti path. It is the act of bestowing spiritual power upon the disciple when the time is right and when the disciple can be considered fit and worthy to receive. When the disciple can hold the powerful energy and not misuse it, it can happen that he wakes up and suddenly is filled with power. The disciple may have the power to convince people, to persuade, to heal, to give and to make people strong and to get what he wants. That is shakti path; you may say something, make some kind of a statement or request and everyone will comply without question. Shakti path is like power falling upon you - like apples from a tree. Mystical power is amazing.

A spiritual initiation is a mystical experience. It is private and individual, rather than collective. You should keep that energy confidential as it is sacred and secret. You should preserve and utilize this power to further your own spiritual advancement. The same applies when you are being given a mantra. When a sacred mantra has been given to you personally; it should not be disclosed to anyone. It is for the individual and it is confidential. Therefore, spiritual initiation may be regarded as a rite of passage that takes the aspirant from one level of functioning and from one level of consciousness to the next.

Chapter

28 Questions and Answers

Svamiji's Introduction: Once again we are connected through technology, although you are always connected to Me. Whenever you are able to attune or think, the connection will be there. Spiritually you can connect yourself anytime and anywhere. Whether in physical form or through technology, I am here to respond to some of your questions.

Q: Svamiji, could You please talk to us about how one becomes worthy of Your grace and how does one open up to it.

Svamiji: To become one is something one has to understand from the point of opening your consciousness. You have many layers of consciousness: physical, subtle, psychological and psychical; and you go through them one by one. As you prepare your inner self, antakaran, the inner sanctum of yourself, you come to understand yourself. Then you can establish a connection with your Higher Self, knowing that you are not just your body, senses and desires - or any of the outer layers of your structure. You are connected in the spiritual realm and that connection is established once you have evolved to that state of mind. It is like closing the outer door and seeing the inner door open.

The world has so many distractions, so many contradictions, and so many thoughts and ideas - so much sankalpa creating commitments, intentions and pledges and so much vikalpa, abandoning those pledges, giving up or finding alternatives and substitutes. Mind is always working on the lower level of consciousness; the gravity of mind is earthbound. Once you are able to go beyond that, for instance, when you are extremely happy or conversely in great pain, in a state of extreme emotion or desperation, it can happen that you suddenly connect spiritually quite easily. It is also helpful that at such a time you are focused. If you have knowledge then you can forget the whole world and you can connect yourself and prepare for the higher energy, higher knowledge and higher Grace.

Q: How would someone who is starting the spiritual journey and wants to connect to Your Grace, but has not yet closed the outer chamber and is not in a great state of despair or desperation be able to connect while still having many worldly desires?

Svamiji: Well, that is why I am here; I am sharing Myself with you. When you hear Me, when you listen to Me and when you think of what I have said, contemplating and meditating on the message or when visualizing or looking at an image, you connect with Me. These are the very simple methods of attunement and the first steps before you begin to go deeper toward a higher connection. One by one as you progress you will find yourself attuned. It is the nature of mind to be always thinking since the mind is one of the greatest forces in your system. It resembles the movement of the waves of the ocean, always moving; even the slightest wind will create waves. It is also the nature of water to create waves. And the very nature of mind is to create thought energy, create desires and wishes. The mind constantly creates and recreates, resembling the bubbles of the ocean that are being created and again will merge into the waters of the ocean. Through practice connection can occur while the worldly desires are controlled.

Q: Could you please talk to us about Love, the Divine Love?

Svamiji: Love is a progression; you start with simple care and love, like that for a newborn child. It instinctively knows that it is being taken care of and forms an attachment to the caregiver. A child does not know the definition of love but it shows love and that depth of love is very deep. A baby does not need to explain what love is, it experiences love instead and that love is perceived by the mother. You are overwhelmed by thinking and knowing, and that is how it starts. Love is like a vast ocean and you can dive into it endlessly - as you can into the Supreme Love, the unconditional love which will become bhakti. Narada defines love as being filled with the nectar of immortality. You feel that every part, every cell and every nerve of you is filled and fulfilled with the love of the Divine. The one who finds that kind of love is eternally fulfilled and complete. Comparing the Divine Love with Enlightenment would be an apt comparison.

Ultimate experience of love is like enlightenment. It is falling in love with your Self, the nonphysical Self, the Ultimate Self - your true being. It is a process of unconditional discovery. People often make the statement that they love God without knowing what God is. Only when you have an understanding of your own ultimate reality God is not far from you. This is not the common human love, but it is a profound understanding of your Self. It is an infinite experience. Ultimately, when you are discovering your own Being, your own Self, then you are nearer to the ultimate Supreme Being - you may call it God.

Q: Svamiji, could you explain the real difference between religion and true spirituality?

Svamiji: Religion prepares the ground for you to stand, teaching you the basic tenets. But a time will come when you alone are responsible for your own religion and for advancing into spirituality. It is a process of what you have learned, and now you are breaking free from the dogma of your particular religion/culture. You could liken it to the shedding of a snake's skin. Established religion may serve a purpose and give you a lot of help and support, but it has its limitations. It is like getting a foundation of learning in school and college and then advancing towards a PhD. Consider religion as a stepping stone, for without positive belief the concept of a Higher Being may be difficult for someone to comprehend. Religion gives you a sense of direction. However, once you are able to walk, you have to walk alone. You take responsibility for yourself and for your further growth.

Q: Svamiji, you had mentioned the difference between compassion and Grace; compassion being a universal energy and Grace being more individual.

Svamiji: Compassion is like sunshine and that is the only thing a High Being can afford to have, compassion for everyone. They cannot afford to be angry - the anger of a High Being can destroy the world. There is a story of Lord Rama, that one angry look would be enough to destroy the world - and yet He is crying, searching for Sita, acting human and helpless. On that highest realm there cannot be anger, only compassion, like the famous compassion of Buddha.

Q: What actually brings Grace, what qualities in the seeker would elicit grace?

Svamiji: Grace is a very individual energy. When someone is really trying to evolve, Grace will be there, like trying so very hard to achieve something. I give you one example of what grace is: One Seabird was very distressed at the seaside. A great High Being was passing by and saw the anguish of the little creature and asked: "Why are you so upset little bird?" The bird replied: "The ocean has destroyed my nest, my eggs, my children and I have to destroy the ocean now." The High Being said: "Do not be distressed little bird, I will help you". He took the ocean into his hands and drank it, allowing the little bird to lay its eggs and raise its young.

That is called Grace: when you are trying very hard and deserve - not just desire. You have to be striving seriously, you cannot just say: I have done my mantra, etc., now give me. That does not work, and you cannot pretend. But when you sincerely strive, Grace energy will come unexpectedly.

Q: Svamiji could you talk to us about sincerity?

Svamiji: Sincerity is when you are true; when what is within you is also what reflects in your attitude. Your whole being, thought, word and action have to be as clear as a mountain lake - where you can count every single stone. The heart needs to be as pure as a child's. A child has not yet learned to be conniving and manipulative - although later they learn that too. The very nature of the heart is true-ness. Only when all three: thought, speech and action match is sincerity evident. If speech, thought and action differ, it can never be sincerity. If you want to have Grace you have to be sincere. It requires purity of heart. As long as there is pretense, Grace cannot enter; you have to empty your vessel, which is already filled with desire. All those elements have to be removed. If you want grace, that is the qualification.

Q: What is the best way of doing contemplation, Svamiji? How can one take all those elements out, how to dissolve the ego? There are so many layers, what is the best way?

Svamiji: When you are on the path of devotion, sadhana and spiritual quest it becomes like a 'melting' process - like when the Sun shines on snow and ice and the ice begins to melt. When you practice the disciplines of sadhana, devotion, humility and knowledge, you do not have to worry about ego, because ego dissolves by itself, by the very nature and energy of devotion and love. It is then that you are ready for contemplation.

Q: How does the seeker develop devotion, bhakti - especially if someone is not naturally inclined to be emotional?

Svamiji: Not only humans but every creature has a longing to be liked. That is part of the very nature of the human being. You want to love and to be loved. Love is the basic instinct in every creature and that has to develop. Eventually it will become more refined, profound and more meaningful.

Q: How does one refine the heart's love and devotion?

Svamiji: By knowing. When you know all the beauty, all the wonderful and extraordinary things, then your heart is spontaneously filled with love. You grow like a flower in the right climate and soil. Knowledge is what makes you want to find out more. When you see a beautiful flower in the field you see the beauty and you are filled with spontaneous love and devotion.

Q: Svamiji, you had mentioned about combining bhakti and knowledge, both complementing each other. Could you talk a little more about that?

Svamiji: Bhakti is like the essence of life and when bhakti meets the great knowledge, it will provide clarity and understanding of yourself. When knowledge combines with bhakti, this will free you from all anxieties, insecurities and fears. Knowledge alone can be very dry, but bhakti is like a catalyst, therefore the two together form a beautiful package - and service, seva and karma yoga become all part of this package. Bhakti involves your heart and knowledge involves the faculty of thinking, the brain, and those faculties which rationalize and have logical conclusions and logical understanding of body, yourself and beyond. If both are practiced together a beautiful manifestation will take place.

You can compare this to nurturing, or preparing the fields. Let us say your fields are dry and you want to plant beautiful flowers, what do you do? First you dig, then you add some fertilizer and water; in short you make it suitable for cultivation. Then you can add the seed which will grow faster and better in this environment. Like this you cultivate bhakti and knowledge. And then knowledge becomes satsang: higher association with truth - association with the High or Divine Being who provides you further knowledge. Or you can employ the practice of ongoing contemplation to provide you with knowledge.

Q: You mentioned seva. The concept of seva as service to the divine principle is very little understood in the west. Could you talk a little about its significance and its power?

Svamiiji: Seva is a very fundamental aspect of the human being. Look at the whole world: everyone is serving you, you are being provided with the wind, the water, the fragrance of flowers, trees that produce the oxygen - they are all doing seva to you and every one on this planet. Then what are you doing? What is your contribution to nature, to Mother Earth, to your community, to your Sat Guru, to your Master, your Teacher, to your family and friends? Seva is an integral part of your practice. How can you say you do not want to do seva? Seva is one of the great methods for purification. In any case, it also gives you fulfillment.

Q: What is the greatest and highest way that a human being can serve in this life?

Svamiji: There are countless aspects of seva, but when someone is distressed and you can help that person that is certainly one of the greatest seva you can offer. To help someone overcome distress or to support a noble cause or to disseminate the knowledge is a great service. There is nothing to lose and everything to gain; why would one not do service or seva? In modern times it has become very difficult to serve or to help anyone, because humans have made it like that by their own limited understanding. It is the collective human consciousness that has brought about the insensitivity toward the distress and suffering of others.

Q: Svamiji, there is a question that many people wonder about; it also seems that it prevents some from seriously seeking the path. They have been told that there is One Divine and yet the world is so full of negativity, violence and darkness. How can these two co-exist?

Svamiji: Quite simply because duality is part of the world. that means that you have darkness and light, day and night and that duality is always present. It is the nature of samsara, the world, and thus it has become the nature of the human being. The world is made of dark and light, good and bad - and even that is relative. Again it is the responsibility of the human being to choose which tendency to follow. If you choose the light, you will have light and if you choose darkness you will have to accept the consequences of your choice. Actually, it is a great freedom that you have so much choice. Darkness, however, is also a great force and the temptation to fall into darkness can be considerable, especially if you want to assert your ego, then darkness appears as support. It does not take much effort to engage in darkness, the trend is downwards, destruction is easily achieved. To create love instead takes time, whereas anger can come in a flash. When you observe all the prevailing negative forces it may seem that such influences are more powerful, but that does not mean that they actually are. The temptation to get caught into darkness is greater for those who have no real understanding of themselves and the higher knowledge.

Q: Svamiji, could you please explain karma?

Svamiji: Well, whatever you do is karma. You have accumulated karma in the past and you are creating karma now, every day. Combining the balance sheet of past and present karma will decide the future course of your life; it becomes the lump sum of your destiny. There is no escaping karma; you continually create it, both bad and good. Karma is the very nature of this physical body for all - except for those who are not attached to their actions.

Q: Is there a best way of not identifying with one's actions, of not being the doer?

Svamiji: When you establish that you are the doer you must take responsibility for everything. Yet when you become an observer, you become much more neutral and you do not associate yourself with those elements that are taking place anyway. When you detach yourself and do not see yourself as the doer, there will also be no karmic repercussions.

Q: What practices would be helpful to cultivate the sense of just being an observer?

Svamiji: Constantly reminding yourself that you are an observer, remembering the knowledge and reminding yourself of this persistently - because forgetfulness is another part of human nature! That is why people who are supposed to love each other have the habit of telling each other 'I love you, I love you ' although at times this is no more than just rhetoric. Reminding yourself has its uses: 'I am not the body, I am not the senses, I am not my anger, desires, frustration or depression. My body is my vehicle and my means to achieve.' It is good to remind yourself rather than have someone else remind you of some behaviour or flaw, because that can be painful and may elicit a strong reaction. You may defend, justify and emotionally argue the point that has been made.

I usually do not like to remind or correct anyone personally, except in my talks. I have made it a rule not to correct anyone; my doing so would have much more impact on emotional upheavals and crises. Instead I would like people to learn from my talks so they can remind themselves, to detect any problems and proceed to correct themselves. The ability to detect and remove problems is the capability you have to acquire in order to purify. Thus you become your own teacher. You can look at your own thoughts, emotions and manifestation and ask 'where did I go wrong?' Self-correction is the method to grow.

The Glossary

antakaran	the inner sanctum of yourself
antarang	internal aspect of human being
arati	ritual in which the seeker offers himself and beseeches God or Sat Guru to relieve him of the distress and afflictions of the world
Atma (n)	the Self, the Immortal Soul
atmik	adjective referring to the Atma
Akasa	sky, ether, free space, beyond earth
Akashik Records	non-physical "library" of all that has been and is, representing individual and collective cosmic consciousness of thought, word and action
Arjuna	Receiver of Knowledge in the Bhagavad Gita - friend and disciple of Krishna who reveals the sacred knowledge while on the battlefield of Kurukshetra
Ashram	Training school for spiritual aspirants - centre for learning and growing under guidance of bona fide Guru and spiritual retreat
Ayurveda	"Knowledge of Life" - ancient science of health

	management, initiated by Sage Dhanavantri based on the law of nature and body politics
Bhagavad Gita	"The Divine Song" - a celebrated mystical poem of 18 chapters, containing the sacred dialogue between Krisna and Arjuna. A major spiritual and philosophical treatise; the source book of Hindu philosophy.
bahirang	external aspect of human being
Brahma	The Creator (see chapter 2, "Developing a Positive Mind")
Brahman	The Supreme, Absolute and Ultimate Reality, the eternal all-pervading, all knowing, changeless Consciousness
Brahmarandhra	the "thousand-petaled lotus" (sahasrara chakra) in the crown of the head
bhajan	devotional song
bhakti	transformed and universal spiritual love and devotion
chandan	sandalwood paste
Chandrama	the full Moon
Damaru	small, hand held drum - associated with Siva in the form of Nataraj while performing the cosmic dance, the Tandava
Durga	warrior aspect of Parvati with ten arms - She is the one who in times of intense distress defeats the demons
Gunas	lit: string or thread - as an abstraction it refers to 'tendencies', to the three subtle qualities, the fundamental operating

	principles or predispositions of prakriti, the universal nature. Each human being is subject to these tools of maya, the great illusion. Creation could not have taken place without these three subtle qualities: • Sattva - the quality of light and positivity • Rajas - the driving force for passion and activity • Tamas - the signature of darkness, inertia and negativity
Guru	gu - darkness; ru - light; the preceptor or spiritual guide who takes you from the darkness of spiritual doubt into the light of true knowledge - the Sat Guru (the highest Guru)
Janaka (King)	King of Mithila - enlightened ruler
Jivatman	the embodied individual soul
Kabir	14th century mystic poet of India revered by Hindus, Sikhs and Moslems alike. Kabir, in his simple, straightforward approach gave a new direction to Indian philosophy.
karma	action, work, deeds, performance, the result of one's actions
Karma Yoga	The yoga of selfless action - not seeking recognition or reward for one's actions
Krisna (Krishna)	Divine Incarnation of Vishnu - stories and teachings associated with Him represent an integral part of Vedic philosophy with applications for daily living

lila	Divine Play, playing one's part in life selflessly
Mantra	concentrated energy of certain sacred sound syllables (see the discourse "Mantras")
Maya	the great illusion of the world as reality; Mother Nature
Mithila	ancient Spiritual Land bordering Himalayas - birthplace of many Enlightened Beings
Narada	also known as Narada Muni with His Vina, is a Divine Sage and ardent devotee of Lord Vishnu, often referred to as the cosmic traveler with the ability to visit distant worlds or planets.
Paramatman	the Ultimate or Supreme Being
Parvati	the Divine Consort of Siva - incarnation of the Divine Mother
Prana	Vital Life Force, also Breath of Life
Prasad	lit: gift of grace - anything, usually edible, and sanctified
Purna	Purna (Whole) is derived from root "Pri" meaning to fill. Thus Purna means full or complete. Purna can also be interpreted to mean infinity, totality and completeness.
Puranas	Ancient scriptures teaching spiritual principles and values through the medium of stories and legends about Deities and High Beings
roti	Indian unleavened flat bread
sadhana	spiritual practice

Sadhu	seeker of truth - travelling mendicant
Sanskrit	most ancient, totally logical language - still in active use; root of present Indo Aryan languages, language of God
Satsang	sat - truth, sanga - company; lit: "higher association with Truth." Keeping attuned with Saints, Enlightened Beings and their teachings
saswath	always new, perennially intoxicating, new and joyful
sankalpa	desires, wishes, intentions with determination, commitments
sanyasa	renunciation in fullness – from desires and attractions
Shakti	Power, energy, the Divine Power of Cosmic Energy
Seva	selfless service without expectation of recognition or reward
Surya	the Sun
Tandava	Siva's cosmic dance of creation and dissolution
Tulsidas	Gosvami Tulsidas, Indian poet and philosopher/saint
Vedas	lit: true knowledge; ancient, sacred texts of Civilization, consisting of 4 collections: Rigveda - dealing with true knowledge Samveda- devotional and ritual songs Yayurveda - dealing with aspects of health and medicine Atharvaveda - dealing with the aspects of Nature

Vedanta	system of knowledge based on the essence of the Vedas, concerning the nature and relationships of 3 principles: 1. the Ultimate Principle; 2. the world; and 3. the individual soul
Yayurveda	see Vedas
vikalpa	vacillations of mind- giving up your pledges and commitments - finding alternatives and substitutes
viveka	discrimination on the basis of foregone investigation, resulting in true knowledge
Yagna	Ceremony of Offering as a means of invoking energy of High Beings - also fire ceremony -celebration and discovery of Knowledge
yoga	lit: union; derived from the root YUK, meaning "to join" also translates as "yoke" impulses and inclinations of the ever wavering mind are brought under the discriminating yoke of the Higher Self. There are different types of yoga, each starting with a different aspect - all leading towards harmony and integration of the whole being.
Yuga	Age or cycle of time - the four yugas - (see "Concept of the Guru and the Phases of Time", chapter 10).

Note: Please also refer to the text for more terms and definitions.